totally fine

(and other lies I've told myself)

tiffany philippou

Thread

Published by Thread in 2022

An imprint of Storyfire Ltd.
Carmelite House
50 Victoria Embankment
London EC4Y 0DZ

www.thread-books.com

ISBN: 978-1-90977-072-0
eBook ISBN: 978-1-80019-750-3

Printed and bound in Great Britain

The FSC® label means that materials used for the product
have been responsibly sourced.

This book includes references to suicide; please take care when reading and reach out for help if you need support. There are some resources at the back of this book.

Some names and other details have been changed to protect identities.

To 'The Annas': Anna Codrea-Rado and Anna Steadman
I feel like I can do anything with you by my side.

The role of a writer is not to say what we can all say,
but what we are unable to say.

— Anaïs Nin

Introduction

Do you have a story that you are scared to tell? A story buried so deep inside you that it has become a part of who you are today. A story that you've spent the rest of your life trying to escape. I'm going to tell you mine. This is the story I don't want to tell. It starts in the summer of 2008, shortly after my twentieth birthday. I was a student at Bristol University and about to begin my final year of a history degree before venturing out into the promises of the real world.

One day that summer, I was sat in a front-facing window seat on a train, travelling back to London from a weekend of partying with my best friend, Anna C., in Durham, when I received a phone call that suddenly changed everything. I was told my boyfriend Richard was in hospital. Earlier that day, Richard was at his parents' house in a suburb near Reading when he opened a letter from Bristol University. The letter told him that he'd failed his retakes and would have to leave the university. Richard read the letter, walked into the garage of his parents' house and hanged himself. He died seven days later. I spent most of my twenties pretending this never happened.

Brené Brown, a professor at the University of Houston, shot to fame at around this time, but I only discovered her some years later. When I finally did come across her, I learned that I wasn't alone in needing to learn from her research. Over 60 million people have watched her 2010 and 2012 TED talks on 'the power of vulnerability' and 'listening to shame'. Brown defines shame as 'the intensely painful feeling or experience of believing that we are flawed and therefore unworthy of love and belonging – something we've experienced, done, or failed to do makes us unworthy of connection.' She says, 'speaking shame is important because its survival depends on being undetected'.

Breaking my own silence happened almost by accident. I met up with an old friend who suggested that I might consider writing a memoir about my experiences of working in startup companies. He recommended a Saturday morning memoir and life-writing course at Goldsmiths, University of London; I signed up that same day.

On my first day, I announced to the class that I was thinking about writing a startup memoir: '*Lean In* for the new generation' is what everyone would have heard. In the last week of the course, when I read my first chapter out loud, the class was stunned as the beginning of a very different story came out of my mouth: the story that's in front of you now.

I'd spent a decade trapped within my own silence, isolated in my grief and left alone to absorb the discomfort and judgement of others that I felt after Richard's death. Once I started to speak my shame, I couldn't stop. I began to explore with brutal honesty what had happened to Richard. It took me to a level of understanding of him that went deeper than I could ever have imagined. I learned that my own struggles during my twenties mirrored his feelings of isolation before he died. I also learned that this story is much bigger than just me and Richard: it's about the expectations of society, and the messages we're given about what matters in life.

My twenties capture a specific era. I was born in the middle of what we now define as 'the millennial generation' and graduated from university in the aftermath of the 2007 financial crisis. We were the internet's guinea pigs – everything online happened to us first, and my twenties coincided with the aggressive rise of social media. But despite this rapidly changing world, my problems as a young person trying to cope with the expectations of society are timeless.

In our twenties, we are thrown into the adult world without a guidebook. It's a decade that should be about adventure and discovery, so why does it feel catastrophic when we fail? How are we expected to have mastered our lives in such a short amount of time? By writing the story of Richard and me, I learned that the turning points in my life occurred at my biggest moments of failure. It was at those points that my shame monster would reveal its nastiness. I want to hug my past self; I want her to have this book.

Suicide is the biggest killer of men under the age of 45 in the UK,[1] and in the time that you've been reading this introduction, four people in the world have died by suicide[2] and 80 people have attempted suicide. By the end of today, 11 men in England and Wales may have died by suicide.[3] The statistics are screaming at us, but we're not listening. For each of those deaths, many loved ones are left behind, but you rarely hear our stories. Perhaps after reading mine, you'll understand why.

---

1 MacKay, H. (2018) 'Male suicide: "His death was the missing piece of the jigsaw".' *BBC Online* (28 March), available at www.bbc.co.uk/news/uk-43572779. Retrieved 8 July 2021.

2 More than 7000,000 people die by suicide every year, which is one person every 40 seconds, and there are indications that for each adult who died by suicide there may have been more than 20 others attempting suicide.
   World Health Organization (2021) 'Suicide data.' Available at www.who.int/teams/mental-health-and-substance-use/suicide-data. Retrieved 8 July 2021.

3 Office for National Statistics (2020) 'Suicides in England and Wales: 2019 registrations.' Available at www.ons.gov.uk/peoplepopulationandcommunity/birthsdeathsandmarriages/deaths/bulletins/suicidesintheunitedkingdom/2019registrations. Retrieved 8 July 2021.

In May 2019, Bristol University made the headlines for the suicide rate among its students,[4] after the thirteenth death in three years. I noticed that one of these students had failed his studies before he died.[5] Something clicked. Here was a parallel with what happened to Richard. Something has gone seriously wrong in our world when failure at university or work can feel so catastrophic to a person that they want to die. Shame is the cruellest of the human emotions, and the further we push it down, the larger it grows. The shame we carry when we fail to reach society's expectations of us is holding us back from a life worth living. Richard was living with a lot of shame before he died. I felt silenced and oppressed by shame once he was gone. Shame is a monster that grows inside us. We all have that monster; it's what we decide to do with it that determines how we live our lives. I wrote to mine.

It has taken me many years to be able to tell this story, just as it has taken me many years to understand that there is no right way to grieve and no right way to live. We must embrace our pasts, even if they make us feel all icky inside, because they are what make us who we are.

Perhaps you have recently lost someone to suicide, or you're about to embark on the rollercoaster that is your twenties. Maybe you're anxiously clutching onto your phone like Gollum with the ring, waiting for someone you like to text you back. Or maybe you're still grieving for someone, decades after they're gone. You

---

4 Stubley, P. (2019) 'Chemistry student dies suddenly in 13th suspected suicide at Bristol University in three years.' *Independent* (10 August), available at www.independent.co.uk/news/uk/home-news/student-death-suicide-bristol-university-maria-stancliffe-cook-a9051606.html. Retrieved 8 July 2021.

5 Morris, S. (2019) 'Bristol told student to leave before he fell to his death, inquest told.' *The Guardian* (1 May), available at www.theguardian.com/education/2019/may/01/bristol-university-student-benjamin-murray-death-dismissed-course-inquest. Retrieved 8 July 2021.

might have been fired from your job, or you didn't make the time to see a loved one before they died. Perhaps you're frightened that you'll never love at all or that you don't know what love feels like and you might let it pass you by.

The need to break our silence and to confront our shame is urgent. It is only by sharing our stories that we can give a voice to the unspoken. If we speak our shame, we can inspire the change we so desperately need, so that we are all free to truly live. Whatever pain you're holding on to, I'm writing this for you.

Part One

Loving

Chapter One

Scribbling in the Sky

'To your knowledge, has he ever had sex with a man?'

'No.'

'What about anal sex?'

'Um, yes.'

'What about drug use?'

'Um, not like the proper ones, like a bit of weed, MDMA, very occasionally I guess.'

'Intravenous drugs? Heroin, needles, anything like that?'

'No.'

'And his parents said that you spoke about organ donation and know that's what he would have wanted. Is that right?'

'Yes.'

'Including eyes?'

'Yes.'

'Okay. We're just waiting for the specialist surgeon to arrive from another hospital – we need to operate as soon as the machines are turned off. We should be doing that late afternoon or early evening. You can go into the room before his family and say goodbye.'

Earlier that morning, I'd arrived at the hospital, leaving my dad in the waiting area – he never came inside the intensive care unit. Richard's parents took me to an empty room and told me Richard had signed up to the organ donation register when he was only 11 years old and his brother was ill. Sweet child.

'We wanted to ask you,' his mother whispered, 'if you knew that's what he still would have wanted.'

'Yes,' I said instantly. 'Definitely, yes.'

I wonder if he knew, as he walked into the garage at his parents' house that morning, that in taking his own life he'd be giving seven people back theirs.

Five days earlier, at 10 a.m., my phone buzzed. I reached over my sleeping friend Anna C., who I'd come up to Durham University to visit for a night out. Richard had wanted to join me, but I was craving some independence. The university holidays had just begun, and a carefree summer stretched out before us.

The text read:

I love you

I often think of that moment and wonder what would have happened if I'd responded differently. I read the text, smiled, rolled over, and shut my eyes. I fell back into a deep and restful sleep, for what would be the last time for a long time.

Anna C. and I eventually woke up around midday. I waited until the afternoon to reply to the text. I apologised for my hungover-induced freak-out about our planned trip to Exit Festival in Serbia that summer. I told him I loved him too. I got on the train at Durham station and rested my head against the window, hoping the nausea would subside.

My friend Dean called me. He said he'd got a call from Richard's work, telling him that Richard had been in a car accident and was in hospital. *I knew.* Dean told me to get off the train at Reading, where he'd meet me and drive me to the hospital. I had four hours left on that train.

'You alright, love?' the train conductor asked. I was bawling.

'Yes, I'm fine,' I said.

'I'm fine' would be the tone of my grief for the next ten years.

Dean collected me and drove me to the hospital. Richard's parents met us at the car. His mum took me by the arm and told me what had happened as we walked in. She couldn't utter the words, so drew a line across her neck with her finger.

The next thing I knew, my mother was standing next to me by Richard's bed in intensive care. She took a sharp intake of breath, covered her mouth and started crying. It was then that I realised the seriousness of what was in front of me. My parents drove me home that night. I texted my friends to tell them that Richard and I wouldn't be going to Exit Festival.

The day that the doctor asked me about anal sex, just minutes after I had learned Richard was going to die, was a Friday. I suppose, technically, I'd had some warning. On Wednesday, the doctors told me he wasn't coming back, that his brain damage was irreparable. They didn't tell me he was definitely going, just that he wasn't coming back. On Thursday, hope had remained inside me, as the cheery nurse yapped away to him as she brushed his teeth. I sat in silence. His hand moved. She said he was responding. I genuinely believed this meant the doctors had got it wrong and he was coming back. She said it was a good sign – or at least, that's what I heard.

Every day for a week, I sat in silence looking at him. We were surrounded by elderly people and their visiting families. The nurses told me to speak to him, but I was far too self-conscious, and I didn't really have anything to say.

On one of those days, a middle-aged woman came up to me as I was leaving and said, 'They're amazing in there. They fixed our father back to health.' I just smiled, too polite to tell her they had already told me that my boy wasn't getting fixed.

For Richard's final hours, they moved him into his own room. I still couldn't speak out loud as I stood there alone, staring at him.

The deep scar around his neck pulsated back at me, reminding me what he had done. The stringent hospital smell lingered in my nose. 'I will always love you,' I said in my head. I turned around and walked out without turning back. My dad followed me out to the car and we drove back down the M4 to London. The whole way, I kept restlessly flicking between radio stations, trying to find the right song.

I was sat at the kitchen table. Some friends were round and we were having dinner. I left the room to take the call. I came back into the kitchen and announced to the room, 'They've turned off the machines; Richard is dead.' No one said a word and I sat back at my place at the table. I felt numb and all eyes were on me for a reaction that I wasn't giving. There'd been so many stages to Richard's dying – from the call telling me that he was in hospital, to when I was told by the doctors that he'd be permanently brain damaged, to that morning when they said that they were turning off the machines – that I felt numb to this final piece of news. It was like the closing chapter, rather than the dramatic plot twist the other pieces of news had been. I said nothing as dinner continued and plates were passed around the table. I have no idea what me and my friends talked about that night when we went to the local pub, although I do remember which table we sat at.

The next morning, I woke up and came down to breakfast. 'You'll need a new outfit,' my mother said. The next thing I knew, we were in Brent Cross shopping centre and I was standing in the changing room of Jigsaw, wearing a beautiful black dress which still hangs in my wardrobe. The dress looked great – it had a deep V-neck and came in at the waist, suiting my figure perfectly. It was also a size eight. I had always wanted to be a size eight – who knew grief was such an effective diet? Someone later told me that divorce works similar wonders.

I started crying in the changing room and the shop assistant asked if I was okay. My mother barged in. 'She's fine.'

'I shouldn't be doing this,' I mumbled. I pulled myself together.

On our way out, I reached for my phone to text Richard, but then I remembered he wouldn't be on the other end. I put my phone back in my pocket and we went home.

We had to wait a few weeks until the funeral, and the time passed in a blur. I was in a daze most of the time, and on anti-nausea drugs because my anxiety was so severe. I also kept breaking out in itchy hives down my legs and had to take antihistamines, which knocked me out.

When it came to offering sympathy, people were a bit crap. The head-tilting was the worst. I hated the pity. I hated the surprise on people's faces if I attended a group event – as if they thought I should be at home mourning and that I was ruining everyone's fun by bringing my misery to the party.

My mother took me to the doctor. I declined the offer of antidepressants. The GP handed me a slip for three free counselling sessions. Wordlessly, I threw it in the bin on the way out; I didn't want counselling, I wanted Richard back. Years later, my mother said to me, 'My friends all say that I should have got you some counselling when Richard died.' I didn't reply. What was there to say? I didn't want to talk about what happened. I wanted to scream over and over again that I wanted him back. It was when I let my guard down and fell asleep that the anger came out. I slept in the bed with my mother most nights because it was too awful to lie there alone and I'd often wake up screaming. Or worse, I'd wake up forgetting what had happened, believing he was alive and then relive the horror as it came back to me that Richard was dead.

My mother bought a book about 'The Five Stages of Grief' and left it on the kitchen table. It sat there glaring at me, a reminder that my pain fitted neatly into a formula. It pissed me off. I felt uncomfortable around my family and thought it would help if I was generous enough to offer up one of them instead: *Please take one of them. Any one of them. Please take them and give me back Richard.* I have no idea who I was talking to. When Richard was alive, but in hospital, I'd got out of bed one night and kneeled down to pray. It hadn't worked.

Richard's parents called and asked me to say some words at the funeral about his time at university. I told them that I didn't know what to say when, in truth, I didn't feel entitled to be able to talk about our time at university. All our time together felt like a lie and I didn't trust my memory or version of events as I still didn't understand how he could have taken his life. I feared getting up in front of people and facing the judgement of others as I talked about our time together because that's what led to his death. My mother didn't question it and suggested I read a poem instead. We pulled out all the poetry books we had in the house. We had a lot. My mother had been an English teacher for over 30 years. Anna S. came round and we took half the books upstairs to my room, leaving my mother in the kitchen with the other half. I lay on my bed while Anna, the fastest reader I know, went through them, turning down the corners of anything suitable before handing them to me to review. I'd never particularly liked poetry at school.

'What about the *Four Weddings* one?'

'We probably can't do that one,' Anna S. said. We burst out laughing.

We eventually found something neutral and appropriate. But years later, on New Year's Day 2017, I'd be wrapped in my duvet in the flat that Anna S. and I shared, a Domino's pizza box by my side, when John Hannah appeared on the screen: 'Stop all the clocks.' I smiled to myself, recalling that moment of hilarity all those years ago. It's a shame I couldn't read that poem. It really is a good one.

'Scribbling on the sky the message He is Dead.'

*

When the day of the funeral arrived, I put on my new dress and a pair of black high-heeled shoes that I'd bought in the sale. They were one size too big, so I wore them with insoles. I looked at my reflection in the mirror and felt frustrated that I had a spot on my right cheek. I'd wanted to look perfect.

Once I was outside, I put on Anna S.'s tortoise-shell Ray-Bans. A few days earlier, she had taken them off her head and handed them to me in the pub when I'd lamented that my yellow sunglasses weren't going to look right for the occasion.

When we were hanging around outside the crematorium before the service, my friend Molly came up to me and said, 'You look like Jackie O.' I smiled, and with my dark shoulder-length hair and side fringe, I found comfort in suspending myself from the pain of my current reality and into the persona of Jackie O, I thought that yes, I did.

The cause of Richard's death hovered above the funeral service, unspoken. Some of his school friends had turned away from me when I'd tried to say hello before we'd gone inside – they would delete me as a friend on Facebook soon after. The two Annas and a couple of my other close friends formed a guard around me. I walked in with them and we sat together in the second row.

During the wake, one of our Bristol housemates, Zac, asked if I wanted to go out for a cigarette. I scanned the room to check that my parents were occupied and found a small thrill in the escape.

'I don't trust Zac,' Richard once said to me.

'Really? Why?' I replied. He was never able to articulate a solid reason beyond a feeling, and it wouldn't be long until I'd understand what he may have meant by it.

It was pouring with rain, so we lit our cigarettes and huddled in the doorway of Richard's parents' house. My dad came outside and saw us and said nothing. I yearned for the simpler carefree times of our French summer holidays when my dad would search me for cigarettes before I left the mobile home. I'd outsmart him by giving Anna S. our cigarettes to carry, knowing that he couldn't search her. At the campsite's bar, we'd laugh in a cloud of smoke, delighted at our cunning.

When it was time to go, I went to say goodbye to Richard's parents. We looked into each other's eyes and none of us spoke for a moment. We said goodbye and they wished me all the best. It was the last time we saw each other.

'You worked the room really well at the funeral,' a friend told me the next day.

I thought, that yes, yes, I did.

Chapter Two

Red Was Our Colour

Let's go back to the beginning. It was September 2006 and I was 18 years old and on my way to Bristol University. I was excited to start this new chapter in my life as I rolled up in my parents' car at Goldney Hall, my student accommodation for the next year, and a beautiful setting for this tale to begin.

There are three people I remember meeting on my first night at university. The first was Evi, who would teach me how to cook a jacket potato. I'd chosen self-catered halls because I couldn't stand the idea of canteen food and prided myself on my independence, but the reality was my big sister had made my dinners on most nights after school and so I wasn't as independent as I'd thought.

Self-catering meant we were divided into flats of eight and we'd share one kitchen. I took an instant dislike, without fair reason, to the people I was put in a flat with, but our instincts are strong when we're young and the feeling was mutual. On the first night, welcome drinks were at the Goldney Hall bar. I ditched my flatmates as soon we got there and headed outside. I spotted a cool, artistic-looking girl with flaming red hair. I made a beeline for her and asked her for a light.

'Sure, what block are you in?' she asked, in a soft Northern accent.

'Oh, I'm in J Block. I don't really like the people in my flat, though. Will you be my friend?'

She laughed kindly. 'Don't worry, I'm on the third floor of A Block, just across the way,' she said. 'We've got some great people and we've made friends with the boys in the flat below. Come up and meet everyone once we're done here.'

'Thanks – you're a life-saver.'

We spent the night chain-smoking outside, pausing only to run up to the bar to get snakebites – a disgusting combination of beer, cider and blackcurrant cordial, which was the signature cocktail of Freshers' Week. We drunkenly swapped stories of our lives until this moment. Evi had been on a gap year in Thailand, while I'd been to Newquay and the Edinburgh Festival over the summer. To me, she was exotic, wonderful and like no one I'd ever met. I felt safe in her presence.

After the bar closed, we headed up to Evi's flat to carry on drinking. We made our way through cans of cheap cider and smoked cigarettes out of the kitchen window. While we were sitting at the kitchen table, a tall, fair boy came in and walked straight to the fridge. He seemed grumpy and wasn't particularly keen to talk to us, but my interest was piqued. Evi, whose social ease I envied, introduced him: 'This is Richard.' He mumbled 'Hi' and kept staring into the fridge. He finally grabbed a beer and then stood by the fridge, clutching his beer can.

'He does computer science,' Evi continued.

'Nice, can you help me set up my computer?' I thought I was being hilarious.

'That's not what computer science is,' he said, before leaving the kitchen.

This would be our first and our last conversation about his course.

Shortly after that, a good-looking boy with a shadow of a beard and wearing a grey Gap hoodie joined us at the kitchen table.

'I'm Zac. I live downstairs,' he said.

'Evi has adopted me because I hate my flat,' I replied. 'Where are you from?'

'London.'

'Oh, me too. Whereabouts?'

It didn't take long for us to discover that he'd gone to one of the schools we'd source boys from. Often the coolest ones too. We knew some of the same people. He was best friends with a friend I'd made at the school debating championships earlier that year. Talking to him reminded me of home.

My first few days at university didn't go well. It didn't cross my mind that I'd have trouble making friends. At my all-girls school, even though I sometimes felt different from the others, I had a good group of friends. My mother was Irish and my dad Greek-Cypriot, so I neither felt fully part of one of those cultures or the English culture either. Our home was a cultural mishmash and I'd be reminded of it whenever I'd go to friends' houses and look on in awe as we were fed food I didn't have in my house, like fish fingers and oven chips.

So after those bumpy first few days, I settled into my tribe, a group dominated by Londoners and boys. We were a mix of people from Evi's flat, the one below and a boy, Daneal, who I'd met on A-level results night when I'd gone out without knowing if I'd got into Bristol because I'd missed my grades.

'You made it in then?'

'Just about.'

Sometimes, I wish Bristol hadn't let me in.

My bedroom was smaller than the others, but it was the social hub because I let people smoke in it. I preferred to host, fearing the rejection of knocking on someone's door and being told to go away; no one else seemed to suffer from this anxiety, so I constantly had visitors. I'd stuck a *Breakfast at Tiffany's* poster on the back of my door; I hadn't read or seen it, but I liked that it had my name.

I stuck fuzzy, printed-out photos of me and my school friends on my bedroom walls with Blu Tack. I still missed the ease of my previous life.

I tried desperately to play cool music when people were round and I thought pop music was too mainstream for my new life. One evening, Zac came by. 'It's so *you* to be playing The Smiths,' he smirked. I was dying to know what he meant by that, but I didn't dare ask.

The boys would be outraged that I played music out of my computer speakers, but I didn't know real speakers were a thing. The first present Richard gave me would be a set of big, red speakers. Red was my favourite colour back then, and red would be a running theme in his gifts to me. For my birthday, I got a red digital camera. The last present he bought me was a red weekend bag. When I thought he'd driven into a wall, in my mind the car was red. Red was our colour.

We enthusiastically embraced the fancy dress themes of Freshers' Week, going all-out on pirate night, pink night, school girl night and, I'm ashamed to say, chav night. Richard warmed up a lot after our first meeting and we got on well and I thought he had a wonderful, strong and soulful laugh. The sound of his laugh is the memory of him that comes back to visit me most often.

One day, when Evi and I were outside having a cigarette, she told me that she'd kissed Daneal, the boy in the flat below me. 'I think Richard likes you,' she then said. I felt excited by the thought that a boy liked me, but I was unsure how I felt about him. Over time, it became obvious that Evi was right as Richard was always around and even if he was talking to someone else, I could sense his attention was on me. Thanks to the intensity of the Freshers' Week social calendar, it only took a couple of themed nights before it was natural for us to be together the whole time. We'd go to the bar together, take time out from dancing in the club to sit down, and there was a calm to our closeness as we chatted away. By the end of the night, both emboldened by alcohol, we'd be so close we'd be touching and I'd lean on him and steal his chips as we'd walk up Park Street back home to our halls. By the second week of term, after one night out, he came up to my room and even though this moment had been inevitable, I felt nervous. I stopped, turned around, looked at him and we kissed. We drunkenly passed out, he came back to my room the following night and shortly after that, without any discussion or fanfare, we were in a relationship.

We spent every night together in my single bed and said 'I love you' within weeks – we couldn't get enough of each other. I loved my little life – I was satisfied with our friends and, finally, I was in a place I could call home.

The first thing Richard would hide from me was his virginity. After a few failed attempts at sex, he'd admit the truth, but I didn't care at all. It liberated me of my own fears around not being sexually experienced enough to be at university. I'd spent a youth feeling anxious around boys and worrying about what they thought of me – I had no idea that men had any problems at all. We were told men have it easy. For us women, life is hard.

The times we were apart were brief, but we'd describe them with such pain. I'd send him dramatic Facebook messages, which are still preserved on the platform today:

> *I love you so much. xxx I'm about to fall asleep without you. It will be awful. It will kill me. I hate it so much. I'm speaking to you now. Xxxxxxxxxxxxxxxxxxxxxxxxxxxxxxxxxxxxxxxxxxxxxxxx xxxxxxxxxxxxxxxxxxxxxxxxxxxxxxxxxxxxxxxxxxxxxxxxxxx*

> *I really hate not being with you. Last night after you went away it was like pain...*

> *I miss you and love you. Call me today, whenever you want. I want to speak to you. Xxxxxxxxxxxxxxxxxxxxxx*

*

One of the most excruciating periods we spent apart was over the Christmas holidays. I'd been to Vancouver for the World University Debating Championships, but I was so desperate to get home that I almost ran off the plane to Richard, who was there to meet me. This was the first time I'd been collected at the airport, and it was the best feeling in the world. My heart expanded into my chest as I saw him standing there – I had never been happier to see anyone in my whole life.

I travelled a lot for my work in my twenties and would think back to that moment every time I dragged myself through arrivals, where Richard had once stood waiting for me. I'd then ride the tube home, a long, lonely journey after a sleepless night on a flight.

At Bristol, we had to choose housing for our second year towards the end of our first term. We'd only known each other a matter of weeks, and the scramble to form housing alliances was brutal. There was no question that Richard and I would stick together – it felt natural. He also wanted to live with his best friend from his course, Fin, so we were a three. I'm the only one of that trio who made it to graduation alive.

The student houses in Bristol tend to be big, so we needed more people and we were a lonely trio until Zac came to our rescue. It was Zac who arranged for us to join him and the rest of the boys. We started house-hunting – the three of us: Richard, Fin and me, and the six other boys. We found a nine-bedroom house on Clyde Park in the Redland area of Bristol and agreed that Richard and I would have the biggest and the smallest rooms in the house. We would mostly use the big room; the small one would be for those unlikely times when we might want some space from each other.

Richard and I loved Bristol, and each other, so much that when our first year came to an end, we decided to move into the house early and spend the summer there. We got summer jobs – I became an estate agent and he worked in telesales. While we were at work we'd write on each other's Facebook walls for all to see, about how bored we were and how much we missed each other. I'd drive to his office in between flat viewings, sometimes just for a kiss, or I'd take him his favourite treat – a Crunchie McFlurry.

I was a great estate agent but a terrible driver. I bashed up one side of the Ford KA they gave me to drive between viewings. After that, at the end of each day, I'd pick Richard up and he'd park it for me so only the good side was visible from the estate agent's office.

It was a glorious summer – I loved my life and was proud to show it off. I hosted friends from London in our Bristol house for my nineteenth birthday party. Friends often came up to visit us and life was good. But then Richard received a letter from the university saying that he'd failed his first year and would have to retake it. Everything changed.

Chapter Three

Bird in a Cage

'I can't take this anymore,' I cried.

'I know and I'm sorry. I'll try harder,' Richard replied.

'I just feel like I'm going crazy. You're in bed all day. You're always just here. You only go out if I'm going out. You don't really talk to the boys.'

'I'll change, I promise.'

'I come home and you're crying and I want to help you, I really do, but I just don't know what to do.'

'I understand. I'll stay out of your way more. You won't even notice I'm here.'

'I just feel like I'm trapped in this room with you. I feel trapped and I don't know what to do.'

'I'm sorry.'

'You know what it's like? I feel like I'm in a cage. I'm a bird in a cage and I just want to be free. But I have this weight. Or maybe this other bird in the cage with me. Whatever. But I feel like I'm being dragged down. I feel like I'm going fucking crazy.'

'I know, I'll sort it out. Just don't go like this.'

'Please do sort it out. Because I can't breathe. And I need to breathe. Just, please, do something with your life. I'm so fucking stressed about work, the paper. I'm getting fat. Just everything. I'm so stressed and I can't deal with this anymore. Please, please just sort it out.'

I slammed the door and walked out. I was hungover.

*

I was always hungover. I'd love to blame my excessive drinking on the grief that would hit me later, but the truth is that I'd got the taste for it as a teen. Alcohol was extremely attractive to a teenage girl who wasn't quite sure of herself. The first time I got properly drunk was at a friend's fourteenth birthday party at a Greek restaurant in Camden. As my anxiety melted away with each drink, I felt increasingly free and became the life and soul of the party. I was running around, making jokes and feeling incredible, until I fell over.

In those teenage years, I was always the one who would take things too far. It was me who'd be the drunkest, the most outrageous and the biggest burden on my friends, who would have to hold back my hair while I vomited and pick me up when I was in a state. They did it all unquestioningly and without judgement. By the time I got to university, I was a hardened drinker and didn't need looking after, with a craving for that warm and fuzzy feeling that would wash over me with each drink. After every drink, I'd feel freer, so I'd have another, and then another.

There was no place where binge drinking was more normalised than at Bristol University, and Freshers' Week set the tone. Friendships would be formed on pub crawls and over late-night whiskeys. Intimacy developed through recounting the shared experience of the drunken messiness from the night before. At the student bars, the loud chant of 'DOWN IT FRESHER' could be heard reverberating around the room. Students would bang the table and shout those words, as the willing participant would pour their drink down their neck with relish, followed by a triumphant cheer.

Our social calendars revolved around drinking: Mondays were pound-a-pint night, Tuesdays were two-for-one shots at Vodka Revolution, and so the week would continue. I still shudder with revulsion as I walk past any chain of 'Vodka Revs', as we affectionately called it. Every Tuesday at Vodka Revs, we'd each buy two trays of colourful shots and make our way through them, cheering each other on, until they were done and it was time to go back to the bar for another round.

On one of my first weeks at Bristol, I got so drunk that I passed out in a toilet cubicle. I was still on the floor of the cubicle when the bar closed and my friends were thrown out. Richard battled past the bouncer, calling out, 'My girlfriend's still in there. Let me through.' He came and found me, picked me up off the floor and brought me outside, where everyone was laughing and waiting. The next day, a guy who was on the periphery of the group broke the unspoken code and shamed me for my actions. 'It was so funny last night,' he said. 'After Richard carried you out, you were just hunched over and dribbling on the pavement.' We avoided inviting him out with us again.

As a group, we didn't really have that much in common – drinking was the only thing we knew how to do with each other. We were bound together by those boozy nights, which gave structure to our lives and the silliness of it all was something for us to talk about.

It was only when an outsider came along that a mirror would be held up to our behaviour. My older sister came to visit on the night of the week that the White Harte pub on Park Row had a menu of drinks that were all £1. Our game was to make our way through the menu, starting with beer and finishing with shots. We'd all see how far we could get, and how fast, but my sister asked for a glass of wine. I'd always found her unwillingness to conform deeply weird.

'You can't just have one glass of wine,' I cried out. That one isn't even on the £1 menu.'

'That's okay, I just want this one.'

'But this is what you do – you start at the top and make your way down. If you don't like beer, I'll have yours.'

'But I don't want to.'

'Fine. Suit yourself.' I briefly panicked at how boring the night would now be for her, but I'd stopped worrying about it by the time I'd reached the spirits section of the menu.

I prided myself on my drinking capabilities, which I was told were particularly impressive for a girl. Emboldened by the belief that I was doing some sort of act for feminism, I challenged Dean to a drinking competition at the White Harte. As we made our way through the £1 menu, I was convinced that he'd hit the floor first. I lost. Before we went to the pub, we each drank a bottle of wine. We documented the whole night by taking pictures on our digital cameras and the next day I uploaded an album of the night and called it 'Black Monday'. The final photo in the album is of me lying on the pavement outside the pub, my friends laughing and posing around me with their thumbs up.

My friends from home didn't share this dogged passion for drinking. When Richard was visiting me in London during the holidays, we went out with them one night and Richard and I kept buying rounds of gin and tonics nobody had asked for. When they lamented that they hadn't finished their previous drink, we'd say, 'Just down it.' We were high on the escapism and we wanted everyone else to get on board. But when others pushed back, there were more drinks for us. Richard and I both felt horrifically nauseous on the night bus home from Camden to my parents' house. The journey was so traumatic that to this day the smell of gin and tonic still makes me retch.

And then, there was also the subtler type of drinking – the one that is easier to hide. It's the casual but consistent type, which was more prevalent in our second year. You'd hear the sound of the communal cracking of beer cans opening every day, at 5 p.m. on the dot. And then there'd be another, and another. 'May as well,' someone would say, 'it's a Wednesday.' It was completely normal. We were grown up now that we were second years and living in our own house. We weren't making our way through one-pound menus or trays of shots. A hangover hides itself well if you stay in bed until midday the next day.

So, on the day when I snapped at Richard, made a shitty attempt at what I thought might be tough love and ranted stupid metaphors about birds in cages, I was hungover. I felt cold and cruel when I slammed that door, but I didn't go back in and make amends – I left Richard alone in that room. We'd recently seen a similar scene in a TV show; perhaps I was trying to emulate it. Richard later told me that he'd felt as if I'd given him an ultimatum and told him to sort his life out. He understood, he said, that I wanted what was best for him, but in reality, I was losing control of my emotions.

Over the months, I'd absorbed his sadness, muddled it up inside me and thrown it back up as a disgusting bile of stress. I complained that I was always tired and stressed, screaming that I couldn't handle it anymore. Meanwhile, here was a guy who spent too many hours in bed and who needed to sort his life out. When I apologised later, he was, as always, understanding. He's the only person I've ever known in my whole life who'd respond to my outpourings of fiery rage with cooling water and a measured calmness.

Back then, words such as 'anxiety' and 'depression' were never uttered – they were extreme conditions, which sat in the same camp as heroin addiction and alcoholism and didn't happen to people like us. No, we were stressed, we were hungover, we were often tired and sometimes sad, and that was totally normal.

But something was going wrong, and as the year went by, Richard was slipping away from me. He was like a weak, flickering lightbulb that finally went out when his grandfather died. From that day, he would spend hours and hours in bed, lying face-down in the pillow. He was done.

In that life that we shared, it was easy to drink too much and stay in bed until it was considered an acceptable time to start drinking again. I didn't question why he never went to lectures; I rarely went to any myself. I presumed that he didn't need to go as he was retaking the year – I trusted that he had the situation under control.

The toxicity spread through our house like a virus, and arguments and tension were rife. It would not be unusual of an evening to hear the crashing of plates as someone said something to wind someone up at dinner and the boys tussled in a stupid fight. Small things like bill payments would lead to battles back and forth over Facebook messenger, and I got sick and tired of having to wash up a spoon, plate or pan before I could use it. The house felt like a dark and difficult place, so I took myself out of it and escaped to the offices of the student newspaper.

By the end of my first year, I was a little bored. I needed mental stimulation and my degree wasn't providing it – besides, my academic studies had always served as backdrop to my extra-curricular pursuits. I needed to find a new thing, so I thought I'd apply to be on the editorial team of the student newspaper. I had little interest in journalism or the news, but news editor seemed like the most prestigious job going and so I went for it.

As with debating, the geekier pursuits weren't in high demand at Bristol. I was one of only two people who applied for the role, and the second applicant became my deputy. It was never clear why I was placed one step above him on the hierarchy – he was far more dedicated to the business of news journalism – but so it was that I was appointed news editor of the Bristol University student newspaper, *Epigram*.

In second year, I began spending more and more time at the newspaper's office on the fifth floor of the student union. To say we took our jobs seriously would be an understatement – it was as if we were wrapped up in our own little Fleet Street. We had seven pages to fill with news stories each fortnight and were constantly on the hunt for a good front-page splash. We'd talk obsessively about winning the *Guardian* Student Media Awards and devoured rival student newspapers with relish. We thought what we were doing was so interesting and important that we filmed a behind-the-scenes documentary to showcase life at the paper. In one chilling moment, I look straight at the camera and say, 'The thing is, when something bad happens at Bristol University, say to a student or whatever, of course, it's sad, but our first thought is – we got our story.'

The editor was brilliant and led a complete overhaul of the paper, and by the end of the year we were flooded with applications from wannabe news editors. While my housemates felt like the family I hadn't chosen, at the student newspaper I felt as if I'd found my people. We shared a bond that went beyond drinking, though of course, we did a lot of that together too.

I spent so long staring at the computer screens in that office, editing articles and perfecting the layout of the news pages, that my eyesight started to go. I detested my sudden need to wear glasses; I didn't like how they looked and I'd hate the daily reminder of my inability to see clearly.

When the newspaper stopped for the summer exam period, I needed a new distraction; short of options, I threw myself into my studies. I'd always been happy enough with the grades I could achieve without too much work, a laissez-faire approach that had frustrated my schoolteachers. They would often hold me back after class, looking as if they were in genuine pain, and say, 'You just have so much potential. If only you applied yourself.' The message never made it through.

As a result, I'd never learned how to study efficiently, so my new passion for my studies caused me a huge amount of stress. I cared more about my work than anything else and I'd repeatedly tell Richard that I was worried he'd fuck it up for me. He promised to stay out of my way and that my study needs would come first. I said he couldn't go to bed late and wake up late because it would disturb my sleep. I wanted to wake up early and maximise my study time. Two months before he died, I sent him a message on Facebook:

> *It's kind of like I don't really want a boyfriend for a little while.*

To which he responded:

> *I know, love. I'll stay out of your way as much as possible. It'll be like you don't even have a boyfriend, except when you're stressed and want a cuddle. Which will cheer you up, promise.*

He'd always call me 'love'. He told me he picked it up from his mother, and it's still my favourite term of endearment.

I was a bitch. I couldn't see beyond my own needs and my own stress and he was nothing but understanding. He wrote:

> *I know that it's difficult for you at the moment with work and stuff, and I'm not getting upset by it. I realise that I'll be the second priority, and I'll try my hardest to be good for you. I will really try love, I don't want to piss you off or anything. I'm happy to get up at 8, cos I have lots of work to do next term too. I think I'll put my computer downstairs so I can come and go to lectures without disturbing you, and we'll try not to argue.*
>
> *It won't be as bad as the first term because we both have loads of work, so I won't be sitting around doing nothing. And I don't want to go out or anything because I have no money. Basically, I hope we'll be okay, trust me*
> *Xxxxx*

How could you not have known? I must have known. I did know. We lived together and were in a relationship and throughout the funeral I kept thinking that everyone was thinking that I must have known. The truth was that I did know and yet I also didn't. When I received the call telling me Richard was in hospital, a voice popped into my head and told me that Richard had intended to die. I'd initially heard that Richard had been in a car accident because that's what Richard's parents had told his workplace at first, so that's what Dean had told me. When I heard that he'd been in a car accident, the image of him purposefully driving a red car into a wall appeared before me, and so even though I didn't know the cause of his death, something in me knew that it hadn't been an accident. It's a vision I still see today, but sometimes he's about to drive off a cliff rather that into a wall. Either way, I always see the determined expression on his face.

While I wasn't picking up on the warning signs that were coming from him, my body was trying to get my attention that something was wrong. I was diagnosed with irritable bowel syndrome, a common stomach affliction often caused by stress. I was bloated a lot of the time and would suffer horrible bouts of diarrhoea or days of constipation. Eating had lost its joy, as what followed was so painful. The doctor prescribed me drugs to prevent my body from treating my gut like a stress ball.

My body tried harder to get my attention when it put me in an ambulance on Park Street in Bristol. The day had started as brilliantly ordinary, for there were plenty of normal times among the darker times. Richard and I often enjoyed walking down Park Street and down through the centre of Bristol. We'd stopped at The Boston Tea Party café, shared a slice of carrot cake and sat in the garden and enjoyed the sun on our faces. Richard let me eat most of the icing as it was my favourite part of the cake. We were calm and relaxed and talked about nothing in particular; things we'd liked in the shops we'd been to and where to go to next. We then went into one shop and while Richard was buying a t-shirt, I suddenly felt too hot, stepped outside and passed out in front of the shop. I came to and then I was being walked into an ambulance by the paramedics, leaving Richard on the side of the road. Park Street is a narrow main road on a very steep hill, and the ambulance was blocking half of the road. As I heard the beeping and the commotion of traffic outside, the paramedic was unstrapping me from the blood pressure monitor.

'Bit stressed at the moment are you, dear?'

I could have spoken to this stranger about the dread I was feeling, the worrying thoughts that were creeping into my head, telling me something was wrong, but I stayed quiet and she carried on.

'Exam time, is it?'

'Yes, just the usual student exams stuff. I'm okay to go now.' And back out I went, through the ambulance doors and into the arms of Richard. 'Yeah, they just said I had low blood pressure because I'm stressed about exams,' I told him. 'No biggie.'

If Richard ever spent an unusually long time in the bathroom, dark thoughts about him harming himself would run through my brain. Weirdly, it would always be an image of him cutting himself with tiny nail scissors, but I swept those thoughts to one side. *So dramatic and odd, Tiffany.*

Then there was the most obvious sign, the one that came from Richard himself: the day that he told me he was going to the doctor to explain that he felt as if he had a dark cloud weighing down on his shoulders. I was hopeful that day. I thought he'd come home with some medication that would fix him, but he didn't. He said he'd been told to come back if he felt the same way in a few weeks. This felt like an alarm bell rather than a warning sign, but one that made me feel hopeless. What could I do – force him to go back? The professional had spoken. After he died, I thought about trying to track down that doctor, to let her know what she'd done. It is only now that I think maybe he never went at all.

It was 2016 and I was sat in a therapist's office in North London.

'Perhaps it was just an overreaction? Perhaps that's why he did it?' she suggested. We'd gone over it, over and over again.

'Yes, I suppose so,' I said. 'Although I guess it doesn't matter if that's true or not, as long as it's a story that I can live with, right?'

But it isn't really a story that I can live with.

After Richard died, I couldn't help but think that at least now everyone knew and I was no longer facing this alone. Although it never occurred to me to do anything but face this alone. I didn't think to talk to anybody about it or think that help might exist. I suspect this was a combination of my own denial of what was happening, coupled with the fact that mental health was not something that was widely discussed among students in 2008. At least – and I felt guilty for thinking this – when I was grieving, people knew something was wrong.

On the New Year's Eve before Richard died, I stood up on a chair and declared a toast. 'Everyone, everyone. SHHH. This year. This is the year that I declare that it's the year of good truth. TO THE YEAR OF GOOD TRUTH.'

'TO THE YEAR OF GOOD TRUTH,' came back the chorus.

And sure enough, that would be the year that a truth, albeit it a terrible one, came out.

I'm sure that other people like me, who've been bereaved by suicide, have a mental list of what ifs and if onlys that they could whip out in an instant if asked. What if I'd spoken to someone? What if I'd tried harder to persuade him to get help? What if I hadn't shouted at him all the time? What if I hadn't run off to do that stupid newspaper? But there's one what if that stands out – a choice that I'd had repeated chances to change. My choice to go to Durham that week and to go alone.

Richard asked many, many times if he could come. Exams were over, and I'd done well, so that stress had gone. But I wanted to be independent, and I wanted to go alone. I had a weird paranoia that he liked my friends more than he liked me, an anxiety that I'd bring to all my relationships. I was sick and tired of us being joined at the hip, and of his reliance on me for social engagement. I wanted to feel free. And so off I went to Durham, all by myself. I flew out of my cage, but just hours later I flew into a new one.

I was 20 years old, and death wasn't something I thought about: I almost felt immortal and believed the same of those around me. At no point did I think about Richard being at risk of death. If I'd known the seriousness and urgency of what I was facing, I wouldn't have started arguments demanding that he pulled himself together. I wouldn't have slammed the door in his face. If I'd known that he was going to die, and very soon, in a matter of days, I'd have shown him love and kindness and offered warm words of appreciation. I wouldn't have told him that I wanted to be alone for a couple of days, not knowing I'd be alone without him forever, and I wouldn't have shouted stupid metaphors at him about feeling like birds in cages. If only I'd known that while I was away, exercising the freedom I so craved, Richard would receive a letter from Bristol University saying that he'd failed his course and would have to leave the university. If I'd known what was going to happen, I might have done things differently.

Chapter 4

The Power of the Pen

Richard is dead.
I wish he was still alive.
The nights are long.

The flowers come from people you don't like that much, the Facebook messages offering to go for coffee if you want to talk come from the school friends you haven't spoken to in years and the real friends show up. The best friends keep showing up long after the funeral has passed.

'I'm a widow,' I said to the Annas on a bench in Cherry Tree Woods. I was waving a cigarette in one hand and clutching a lighter in the other.

'Er, I think you have to have been married for that,' Anna S. said.

'For fuck's sake. You know what I mean.'

We laughed darkly, then went quiet again.

'It's mad though, isn't it, to be like, 20 years old and kinda a widow, or whatever the word is. I mean there isn't even a name for what I am right now.'

'Yeah I know. You can call yourself a widow if you want.'

We laughed again, swiftly followed by another silence.

My friends were my saviours during those weeks that followed the funeral. There were a few of them who were just always there. We spent hours and hours, evening upon evening, sat in the garden of The Old White Lion pub in East Finchley, chain-smoking, drinking wine and talking about everything and nothing. These friends and I were in our own world, where we could relax and laugh with each other because they got used to being around me and my grief. The semblance of normality was so good that there'd be moments where I wasn't thinking that Richard was dead. But I found whenever I did let myself forget for a moment that he was dead, my skin would begin to itch and I'd look down at my arms and legs and see I'd broken out in hives again. I'd lean down to pick my handbag off the floor and quietly pop an antihistamine, wash it down with wine and watch the rash quickly dissolve off my skin. It would happen on most evenings in the pub.

Among the space to forget was space to remember. There was the exchange of nods, but no words, as my friend Jack placed in front of me a big bottle of melatonin he'd got from America to help me sleep. Or when Anna C. joined my gym, which was near my house but not hers, so she could come with me to keep me company because we had no idea what to do in a gym. Or when I blurted out to Molly from nowhere that I was heartbroken and she held my hand and said, 'Of course you are', and waited for me to speak again.

The presence of those good friends was so consistently effortless that I forgot that other people existed who couldn't handle my grief. When Rosie and I took a spontaneous trip to Brighton on a sunny day, I got a call from a girl from my history course. She was in floods of tears and she told me that she'd only just found out that Richard was dead. Each of her sobs hurt my head as if I was being hit by a bat. 'Sorry, you're breaking up there, I have to go, I'm in Brighton, bye.' I hung up and never spoke to her again.

The nights were still a problem. I'd lie, staring at the ceiling, begging for some rest and a break from the torture that was knowing

Richard was gone forever. The melatonin helped me sleep, but not enough. If I got to sleep, my dreams would be nightmares, as Richard would haunt me, vividly, every night. Then I'd wake up and realise he was gone and want to go back to the nightmare.

I got used to the tiredness. My brain was slowly being trained out of the habits I'd formed with the person who I'd spoken to the most in the world. I stopped reaching for my phone to text him and, somehow, I slowly made it through each day. I was no longer drowning, but doggy paddling, and my head was being held just high enough above the water to keep going. But the waves of anger would still come, and my sister was my target.

I decided it was her fault because nothing like this would ever happen to her. Inside my chest there was a dragon breathing fire with nowhere for the fire to go and so it built up in me, trapped with the heat and desperate to lash out. This would never happen to you, little miss perfect with your six grade A A-levels, your fluency in four languages and the ease with which you attract men, always. She tried to tell me that she understood loss as she'd felt heartbreak when she broke up with a guy called Davide. I told her to fuck off and threw a ketchup bottle at her. I went up to my attic bedroom and sat by the window sobbing at the unfairness of it all. I now know that my sister was quite right and grief and heartbreak are cruel emotional cousins. After I hurled the bottle at my sister, when my mother got home, she told me it was okay. I knew I'd done something wrong and that was when I realised my grief came with a carte blanche on behaviour, and yet, I could never have the one thing that I wanted.

Anna S.: *Hey, a family in Crouch End are looking for a nanny for summer, interested? xx*

Me: *I don't know, am I? xx*

Anna S.: *I think you should do it. xx*

Me: *Okay, do I need to tell them what happened?* xx

Anna S.: *No, I wouldn't. xx*

I was standing in front of the mother in her kitchen in Crouch End for my brief job interview, feeling weird for not telling her I was a grieving girl with a dead boyfriend. It was so at the forefront of my identity and current existence that it felt wrong not to share it with the mother, yet I did as Anna S. said and didn't mention it because she said it wasn't relevant to my childminding capabilities. Besides, I doubt I could have said it out loud to this woman anyway. Soon after, my dad was driving me on most weekdays to mind a nine-year-old girl and a seven-year-old boy.

Anna S. had always got me my jobs. Our first job together was the best job in the world: at 14, we worked at Brooksby Newsagents in Highgate Village, where we'd eat sweets and read celebrity gossip magazines. Anna S. also got me another job working on the door at Koko nightclub in Camden, where we'd stand side by side, rolling our eyes at the drunk people trying to get in for free because they'd say it was their birthday. Minding the children in Crouch End would be my first job without Anna S., but she was still there, as I'd often text her to ask for childminding advice.

My childminding hours were freedom from my grief. When I arrived at 9 a.m., the children's mother would open the door and call out hello with her back to me as she ran back up the stairs to finish getting ready for work. From the moment I crossed that threshold, I was an adult again. In those children's eyes, I had no past, no future and no dead boyfriend. To them, I was just an adult who had total control over their lives for the day. This meant I had to learn how to make decisions again because kids are constantly asking questions. I was still always tired from restless nights, but the children knew me no other way and so didn't notice. The days would pass easily and I mastered the art of lazy nannying, where I'd add other children into the mix so they could all play among themselves.

'Are you sure you don't mind taking them again?' A frazzled neighbour would say to me as her children were already halfway down the corridor, running off towards the garden.

'No, no, not at all. Please, leave them here for as long as you want. I'm going to take them to the playground later.'

'Thank you, thank you.' She'd say, her back already half turned as she headed quickly down the path.

I'd take my little army to the playground in Crouch End and I'd encourage the kids to exhaust themselves to their hearts' content. I'd sit far away from other parents and childminders, text my friends and intermittently stare off into the distance. The children always wanted to stay in the playground for longer and they'd send the little girl to come and ask me if they could. She was always nervous to ask, even though I always said yes.

I took them to see *Mamma Mia* at the cinema and the little girl loved it so much that we went back to see it again. On the way home from the second viewing, we stopped in the middle of the pavement as she burst into a song and we danced, twirled and I looked up and smiled at the sky.

I was in the park one day with some friends, and Anna C.'s Durham housemate and friend, Melanie, who I'd been friends with at school but hadn't stayed close with, was with us. She mentioned she was planning a trip to Thailand, Cambodia and Vietnam. I felt an urge to go with her because it felt like an escape. We stayed out and ended up in the pub.

'I'd love to do something like that,' I said.

'Why don't you come?'
'Such a fun idea. Let's do it.'

The trip meant that I now had something to work towards and it gave a new purpose to my nannying as I saved the money I earnt. I couldn't wait to get away to somewhere new. I felt a huge amount of satisfaction when we landed in Bangkok and we had a good few days on the Khao San Road. When we got to Cambodia, Melanie started feeling ill and wanted to go home. I loved it and wanted to stay and I felt bad for Melanie and tried my best to comfort her, but I had no capacity to deal with someone else's problems. Back in July, Anna C. had bought me a journal. I hadn't written in it yet – I could barely write after Richard had died. I'd brought the journal with me as I thought it'd be fun to write a travel diary. I went into the hotel bathroom and opened the journal on the first page.

July 2008
Never underestimate the power of the pen,
all my love Anna

19 August

Melanie is ill – nauseous mainly. She wants to go home.
I am not sure if I too want to go home – I want to stay here and see the lovely things and to enjoy this month, but with Melanie being how she is I'm finding it difficult and stressful to be here. The stress is overwhelming and I can't help thinking if Rich was alive and here with me everything would be so much better. Even if I could call him and hear his voice telling me it was going to be alright then that'd be enough.
It makes me so sad to know that I'll never be able to go travelling with Richard, with him this would have been

amazing. We always had such a wonderful time when we went away together.

I often think back to when we went to Prague, what an incredible time we had there. I took a photo of us at Glastonbury together and I'm looking at it now.

I realise that it is not just our holidays that he made so special but every aspect of my life. I miss him so much and it is so hard being without him.

I should not have come here, I realise that now. I did not think how I would feel – I did not know that whenever things were difficult with a friend I wouldn't have Richard to help me. The fact is if Rich was here I would be so happy and having a great time. It is so painful that he is gone. When times are hard here all I can think about is how much I miss Richard. It is so unfair that he is gone. For Melanie, she misses home, she can always catch a flight back. For me, I long for Richard as she longs for home. I do not want to go home as I won't feel any better there.

In whatever I do in my life – be it go to Cambodia or go to Sainsbury's – I will wish that Richard is standing by my side.

In the temple on Sunday in Bangkok we were told to kneel down and make a wish. The words burst into my mind: 'I wish Richard would come back.' I felt like a naughty child as this wish had burst out of me. I realised I had wasted my wish at the lucky Buddha and felt disappointed. I felt guilty for wasting the wish and daring to hope Richard could ever come back.

Tomorrow we plan to just relax in the wonderful four-star hotel we've moved to as a result of Melanie's illness. Hopefully when I wake up I'll be in a better state of mind. Already I feel better for telling you, dear diary, how I feel. I hope I was not too repetitive!

*

Things didn't improve and we decided to leave. I wrote the lessons I'd learned during my brief time in Cambodia.

Wednesday, 20 August

I love Cambodia for the same reason that so far I have enjoyed my life. The people. The people have made my life what it is, have made it worth living.

Today I have learned two things, one happy and one sad. The happy thing is that maybe one day I can obtain happiness and the other lesson is that it is people and nothing else which can cause my happiness.

The loss of Richard is such a dent in my happiness because of the joy he gave me. I did not realise that I was unsatisfied until I met him. He filled me up, it was amazing and I really felt it. It is so painful for me when I admit this and for a moment I think he's still alive.

On my return home I have a lot of work to do. I will have to open up and face how I am feeling. I can only hope that in time it will get easier. I know this pain in me, the longing and sadness, will never leave me. Even when I'm 100 I will yearn for my Richard to come back and just give me one kiss. The thought of living that long without him is too much and so I will go back to focusing on the present.

All I need to do is get through this month. On my return I will have to deal with things. They are burying Richard's ashes – they may have already done it. I cannot wait to visit him and just be with him. I will always love him and he will always be the greatest comfort to me and I am pleased that I will have a place to visit for the rest of my life.

I never did visit him. The lessons were there, right in front of me on the page, but on my return I ignored them and sleep-walked into further avoidance of the truth of my grief, and that avoidance meant I never visited where his ashes were buried. If only I'd kept going back to those words and reading them again. If only I'd continued to write in my diary.

Melanie and I came home and my grand escape was over. My big demonstration to everyone that I was okay and that I could travel and do something positive had failed.

There was only one other time when I picked up the pen.

31 August

I feel very down lately. I don't feel like talking. I'm probably depressed. I just feel so sad that Richard is gone.
I don't want to talk to anyone, do anything or go anywhere.

Most of all, I didn't want to go back to Bristol University.

Chapter 5

Red Wine Stains

'Please don't make me go back.'

My mother stared back at me after I said these words. She was propped up in bed and I was standing by her bedroom door. The tears were tumbling down my cheeks, I'd been crying for hours in my room and I decided that I just couldn't do it. My mouth was quivering, but I repeated myself: 'Please, don't make me go back.'

'Stop,' she replied, looking stern. 'You're going back. That's it.'

'I can't. I can't do it.'

"You're going back.'

I was going back. As summer was drawing to a close, the darkness was coming at an earlier time each day and I became increasingly agitated. On one of my final nights in The Old White Lion, I was sat outside with Molly. Suddenly, she asked, 'Have you thought about changing your relationship status on Facebook?'

I was taken aback. I hadn't thought about it yet.

'No.'

'But you're not in a relationship with Richard anymore.'

I blinked for a moment as I digested this information. I guess I'd skipped the 'it's complicated' bit on the Facebook status update. This was the era when your relationship status on Facebook mattered. It was a rite of passage for any real relationship for the couple to update their Facebook pages to show that they were in a relationship with each other. We'd all get a notification that a couple was now together on our newsfeed, and if we were ever stalking someone's page, we could click through to their partner's page and look at them, too.

I remember being annoyed at Richard for not having Facebook for the first couple of terms of first year and me not being able to add that we were in a relationship, but I also remember when he finally got it and we tagged our status as in a relationship with each other. At Bristol, we'd laugh at stories of people changing their relationship status to 'it's complicated' while a couple were arguing, or at the guy who'd change it to 'it's complicated' before even speaking to the person he was on his way to dump. Changing my Facebook relationship status meant something and it meant a lot. Facebook was the public performance and therefore a reflection of our young lives, and so to delete him from my Facebook page meant that our relationship was truly over. I couldn't bear the thought of it, but I also cared what people thought and I wanted them to think I was fine.

'I'll do it when I get home.'

I got up to get us another bottle of wine. I stared off into the distance and fought back the tears as I stood at the bar.

I reached out and clutched the bottle of white wine that was on the bar. I tightened my grip around it and started to walk back outside to our table. Swaying slightly, I looked up to see a guy walking towards me. I didn't have my glasses on, so only recognised him when we'd both stopped before the door to the garden. It was Luke, who was going to be the student newspaper's sub-editor, which meant we'd be working closely together when we returned to Bristol. I could see Molly watching us through the window.

Luke was tall, thin and had a crooked big nose and dusty blonde messy hair. His sharp features made him both sort of ugly but attractive at the same time. He looked down to the white wine bottle dangling by my side, then up to me:

'That all for you?' He talked as though he was leaning against a wall, even though he wasn't.

'Oh yeah, hi. Well no, I'm with my friend out there and we've got glasses at the table.' I then lifted the white wine bottle and waved it, trying to come across as nonchalant, rather than wasted. I gave him a big grin and titled my head to the side.

'I didn't know you were a fellow North Londoner. How... exciting,' I said.

'Yeah, I live on Orchard Road.'

'No way! I'm on Springfield Road. So, only round the corner.'

'Ha, yeah.'

There was a pause.

'So, I'll see you back for the paper,' I said. I lingered for a moment too long.

'You're going back early, right?' I said.

'Yeh, of course.'

'Well, see you there, if not before.' I resisted the overwhelming drunken urge to wink.

He turned and went back to the other side of the pub. I looked at him walk off, not realising as I saw him go that he'd give me back something. I opened the door to the pub garden and walked back to our table. My little flirty performance had given me a buzz of energy and I sat back at the table, poured our wine glasses up to the brim and lit a cigarette. Molly was beaming, her cheeks were flushed and glowing.

'Who was that?'

'Ah, just the sub-editor for the paper, Luke.'

'He's cute.'

'I dunno, is he?' I looked back through the windows even though he was out of eye view.

'Yeah, maybe. Guess he's kind of gangly.'

I got home that night, hurriedly took my make-up off, leaving black smudges under my eyes and I stumbled up the stairs to my attic bedroom. I opened my laptop, where Facebook was already open on the screen. I went to my profile settings, clicked 'update your relationship status', let the cursor hover for a moment, closed my eyes, breathed in, then quickly removed that I was in a relationship with Richard. My page switched to 'single', his stayed at 'in a relationship', but my name had disappeared from it. I sat there and kept refreshing his page. I was the one who'd gone.

It was September 2008 and it was time to go back to Bristol University for my third and final year. My parents drove me down for the first time since they'd dropped me off at Goldney Hall for the start of my first term. Richard and I had always done the drives up and down to Bristol together in his car. I was irritable and on edge for the whole journey.

I picked up the keys from Fin's work on the way as he'd been living and working there over the summer. We then arrived at the empty house. I hadn't seen the house since we'd signed for it almost ten months ago. We walked through the corridor on the top floor and my parents and I stood in my new little room. It looked horrible and small because it was empty and the bare white walls and uncovered mattress looked uninviting. The bed was pushed against the wall; by the door, at the end of the bed, was a wardrobe and to the right of the bed was a sad-looking desk and chair. The desk was facing the wall that I was sharing with Zac, who was going to be my neighbour this year. As I stood there, I felt pissed off that I had the small room. When I was with Richard, I'd had the biggest room in the house. The other two upstairs rooms went to Zac and Fin. Zac's father had died not long after Richard, and Fin's father had died towards the end of summer, too. So, we were all upstairs together in some sort of grief corridor. As my parents stood in the doorway to my room, I felt overwhelmed with a physical desire to be left alone.

'You can go now.'

'Can we take you to the supermarket or Sainsbury's to buy some things first?'

'No, just go,' I snapped aggressively.

'But we can go and get some loo roll and food and things.'

'No, I'll be fine, I'll just go later. Seriously, just go.'

'Okay.' My mother started to cry as she handed me a wad of cash. They left.

As soon as my parents had gone, I was alone in the big house. I felt guilty for snapping at them and regretful for forcing them to leave so suddenly, but it was such a strong urge that came over me that I hadn't been able to control it. Perhaps I thought that it'd be easier to pretend to be okay about being back if they weren't there, looking on at me with their worried glances. But once they left, the house felt big and empty. This wasn't the house I'd lived in with Richard, and my surroundings were new and unfamiliar. I was alone now, away from my family and home friends, and I felt as if I'd arrived at a place where my grief wasn't welcomed by those who'd I'd now be with. I felt alone and empty like this bare-walled and under-decorated student house. I walked around the house again. There was some crap left around the place, like a lighter on the coffee table and orange squash in the kitchen from when the boys had been there for their room-choosing weekend, but the place looked sparse.

I walked back into my room and sat on the chair by the desk. I decided to make the bed first, as that was the only essential thing I had to do. I then opened my suitcase full of clothes and turned it over onto the bed and it lay there in a massive pile. I didn't have the energy to put it away, so I pushed it to the bottom of the bed and sat resting against the wall with my knees up. I'd acquired a lot of new clothes from recent shopping sprees. I'd maxed out my overdraft for the first time, but I still hated all my clothes. I'd bought a new navy coat as I couldn't bear to wear red anymore.

I texted Oliver, the editor of the student newspaper. I'd come back early to start working on it, so we could launch our new design and layout before the students got back. I mustered all the energy I had to sound as cheery and relaxed as possible. It was important to me that the newspaper, my place of escape, saw me as someone who they wanted to have around and not the grieving, lonely girl that I was.

Hey, I'm here! Xx

He called me back.

'Hi.'

'Hi, how are you?'

'Yeah, good thanks, just got here. Excited to get stuck in.'

'Are you alone?'

'Yeah, no one else is back yet. It's cool I've got lots of unpacking and stuff to do. When's our first meeting?'

'We're having some people round for dinner tonight, do you want to come?'

'Ummm, you sure I wouldn't be gate-crashing?' The thought of other people terrified me but I couldn't think of a reason to say I couldn't go.

'No, come. Nathalie and Luke will be there.'

'Okay cool, text me your address.'

'See you at 8.'

I still couldn't muster the energy to tackle the piles of clothes on my bed, so I put a few of my toiletries in the bathroom and then went back to sit on my bed until it was a reasonable time to start getting ready.

I'd started wearing a lot more eyeliner since Richard had died and I layered on the kohl in the rims of my eyes to prepare for my first social occasion at Bristol after his death. I wanted to look good, to ease my discomfort of going to something where I wouldn't know everyone, but nothing I tried on felt right. I went for a yellow tank top and navy hoodie and jeans. It was still too early to go out so I sat on the chair on my desk and opened my laptop and went on Facebook and looked through the photos I was tagged in until it was time to go.

I googled the directions and drew them out on a piece of paper and pen and set off. I still got lost and had to call Oliver a couple of times, but I finally made it. As I knocked on his front door, I wondered if everyone would know what had happened to me that summer. I couldn't decide which I'd prefer. I was terrified of the question 'How was your summer?'

Everyone else was already there when I arrived. Oliver was cooking in the kitchen and I hovered around him awkwardly. I felt like I had a 'grieving girl' sign around my neck. My jeans felt tight and I kept readjusting how I sat on the chair or stood against the wall. I gulped my red wine, though it wouldn't quench my thirst.

Luke, the student newspaper's sub-editor, who I'd bumped into in the pub the week before, was there and he sat on a chair next to the corner of the sofa I was perching on. I was balancing my paper plate of curry on my knees and resenting letting go of my plastic cup of red wine when I placed it on the floor so I could eat. I wasn't hungry, but I didn't want to leave a full plate of food and so I ate as much and as little as I could without looking weird before getting up and leaving the half-full plate of curry in the kitchen.

I went back to the living room and took my spot on the corner of the sofa again. Oliver came to sit next to me on the sofa and Luke was still sat on my other side on his chair, smoking. Luke gave me his full attention, whereas Oliver would often turn away from me to talk to other people. I kept worrying I wasn't talking enough as I went through long periods of saying nothing during group conversations. My mouth felt dry and I pressed and rubbed my lips together to try and get rid of the red wine stains I knew would be on my mouth.

I didn't want to risk losing my seat sandwiched between people I knew and so I didn't get up to go to the loo, even though I needed to go. Luke seemed to have a never-ending supply of wine bottles by his chair and he kept pouring more into my cup. As the night went on, I spoke more exclusively to him and because I'd hit the chain-smoking portion of the night, I kept leaning towards him to tap my cigarette ash into the tray in front of him. I stopped caring about the red wine stains on my mouth.

'Should we go?' Luke said to me.

'Oh yeah, okay.'

We said our goodbyes and we lit cigarettes as soon as we closed the door behind us.

'Which way?' I said.

'This way.'

'So embarrassing, I got lost on my way here, like so many times.'

'Don't worry, I got you.'

We walked past a stairwell. He suggested we stop at it and sit and have another cigarette. I was drunk and so I started talking about how my boyfriend had killed himself that summer. Luke acted empathetic and let me talk about it – the sorrow, the regret, the shock but how I was, like, totally fine. This was a routine I'd enact in front of many male strangers over the next decade. I'd get wasted, blurt out my story and they'd give me enough empathy back to secure the shag. I felt so seen by these men in these moments, even though it wasn't real. They'd always say, 'I'm so sorry this happened to you.' I believed them so much.

Luke came back to mine. He hovered and picked up the bottle of melatonin I'd left out on the desk in my room for when I got home. I told him about how I'd got these sleeping pills from America, because I couldn't sleep. He turned over the bottle in his hands and asked if he could take a couple. 'I hear they do crazy shit to your dreams,' he said.

Once the sloppy sex was over, I lay there in my new bedroom, staring up to the ceiling and thought that Richard had been dead for less than three months. *You shouldn't have left me, Richard, if you didn't want me to sleep with someone else.* I rolled over and slept through the night for the first time since the day that summer that Richard had gone into hospital.

The next morning, I woke up with the sticky taste in my mouth and a sore throat from all the cigarettes. Luke was sat upright, leaning against the wall and was on his phone. He then did what would grow to be a tiring pattern of putting his guilt on to me. He told me he felt bad about his girlfriend. I didn't respond or engage. He was taking his time about leaving for someone who felt guilty. He finally left. Once he'd gone, I got back into bed. I lay there and I worried what Oliver would think.

The last thing I needed was an obsessive crush. I'd noticed Oliver in second year when Richard was still alive and I was the news editor of the student newspaper and Oliver was the comment editor. He had slightly doughy, wide eyes and sharp cheekbones and a permanent five o'clock shadow. His hair and clothes were messy and yet they fell together well. He was so effortlessly good-looking that I thought only I could see it. Similarly, his personality was so understated that I thought our connection was special. But I thought little of Oliver in second year. He only upgraded his role in my life when it was time for me to apply to be the editor of the paper before the summer of second year. I never considered Oliver would be a threat. He hadn't been in the inner circle of the paper that year and no one took the comment section very seriously. He only laid out two pages that no one read and he wasn't in the office as much as the rest of us who were on the front lines of the news. It also made sense for the news editor to become the editor the following year.

When I arrived for my interview with the current editor and key members of the student union, I could hear Oliver's booming, slightly posh voice coming out of the room. I didn't even know he was applying.

'And how would you deal with the relationship between the union and the student paper?' I heard the head of the student union ask him.

'The paper is for the students and my priority as editor is to put the students first and to tell the truth,' Oliver replied.

That's a good answer. *Damn it*, I thought. *I need to come up with my own answer.* They'll know I've been listening at the door otherwise. I ran away from the door and sat down and waited for him to come out. As he walked out, I gave him a half-smile that said: 'I like your face, but there's no way they're giving that job to the comment editor.'

It was my turn. I walked into the room and sat down on a chair, facing the editor, the sub-editor and a few student union members who were behind a table.

'So, how would you deal with the conflict of interest between the student union and the paper?'

'Well, we get on alright already, don't we?'

I was met with silence as the five of them looked down on their pages and made notes. That sounded so stupid out loud.

'Are you saying that this isn't a potential issue?'

'No, I'm just saying that as news editor for the past year, I am experienced in handling that dynamic and we've never had a problem. We know each other. The lines of communication are open.' They stared back at me.

'And I guess, at the end of the day. It's the students that matter and creating a paper for them...' I trailed off.

'Right. Mmm.'

Rupert, the editor, called me to the student union the next day. We were sat side by side on a sofa outside the main hall.

'So… good news, you've got a job.'

'*A* job?'

'Yes, deputy editor.'

'Deputy?'

'Yes. We gave editor to Oliver. He just did a better job in the interview.'

I stared ahead of me.

'Actually, it's co-deputy. We also gave the deputy position to Nathalie.'

'Sorry, are you fucking kidding me?' I said quietly, staring at the floor, '*Co*-deputy. That's not even a job. You've just made that up. And I have to share it with *Nathalie* of all people. What the fuck? She and Oliver are like best friends. They'll just leave me out of everything. Fuck, Rupert, I can't believe you've done this. After everything this year. After all I've done.'

He sat there uncomfortably. My tears threatened to come, but I breathed them away.

'I'm going to have to think about this.'

'Right, okay.'

There was an uncomfortable silence as I stared into the distance again. Rupert broke the silence.

'Are people often scared of you?' he said.

'What?'

'Can I like get you a tea or something?'

'What did you just mean?'

'Well, you're just very composed right now and it's kind of scary.'

I got up and started walking off.

'I quit. I will not share the job with Nathalie and I will not report to Oliver. Fucking Oliver – I mean – really?'

Rupert looked sheepish as I stormed off.

I got home and Richard was in our bedroom, sitting at his desk. While I'd been cold and composed for Rupert, I unravelled in front of Richard. I lay face down on our bed and started sobbing. I told him I'd quit. I was so sad. I loved the paper. The thought of not having it in third year crushed me. What would I do now? Sit around all day while the boys played *Pro Evo*? It was my lifeline. The paper was the only place I had friends who weren't the ones in my house.

'It means so much to you. You could un-quit. You could still do it,' Richard said.

'NO, NEVER. I DON'T WANT TO.' I mumbled tearfully into the pillow, like a child who hadn't got their way.

'But you could. I think you should.'

My phone started to ring. It was Oliver. I hung up the call.

'FUCK OFF, OLIVER,' I shouted at the phone. Slimy snake. Fuck off. Oliver then texted asking to meet at a pub nearby.

'I think you should go.' Richard said.

'Do you?'

'Yes. Hear him out. You're so upset that you've quit, you never know. It might be alright working with him.'

'Okay. I'll go.'

Yep fine. I can meet you there in 20 minutes.

I picked up a packet of fags from my desk and put my red coat on.

'I don't look like I've been crying do I?'

'No, love. You look great. Let me know how it goes.'

'Thank you. I love you.'

'Love you too.'

'In a bit.'

I chain-smoked as Oliver talked, and stared at him intently while drinking the pint he'd bought me.

'Well, yes, obviously, you'll need me. Doing news isn't like the comment section you know. Do you know how hard it is to find news and fill SEVEN pages at this damn university where fuck all happens aside from a posh idiot trying to replicate the Italian Job by driving their mini down some stairs? And how hard it is trying to think of pictures to illustrate all the boring articles about the student union or whatever. Anyone can just comment on things. The news is the real front lines.'

'I know.'

'And Nathalie? I mean, really? *Co*-deputy. That's just fucking rude.'

'I know I need you and it will be like we're equals. I have a vision for what we can do with the paper next year. And I know Nathalie and I seem close, but it won't feel like her and me versus you, I promise. Please, I really need you.'

'Okay, fine. Fine. Tell me about these grand plans of yours then.' I lit another cigarette and listened to what he had to say.

I was delighted. I couldn't walk away from the paper and Richard was happy for me when I got home. Oliver and I got to work immediately and we started having long phone conversations about our plans for next year as well as general gossiping and silliness. We'd laugh on the phone to each other a lot and I found talking to him addictive and thrilling.

'Who are you on the phone to all the time?'

Zac had come into the smallest room in the house, which had become my study. I was spending more and more time in this little second room of mine and Richard's as the year went on. Zac was swaying. He was often drunk. He flopped on the bed behind me. I spun around.

'Oliver.'

'You're obsessed with Oliver.' He smirked.

'Fuck off, Zac.'

'There's something about him that's not right.'

'You're just jealous because he actually does something that's not playing *Pro Evo*.' As I was facing him, I noticed that Zac and

Oliver looked a bit similar. They had the same skin tone and similar face structure and a permanent five o'clock shadow. They'd also gone to the same school, although Oliver was in the year above. But that was where the similarities ended.

'Sure. It's so awkward how obsessed you are with Oliver.' The boys often teased me about it when Richard wasn't around.

'Go away, Zac. I need to do my work.'

'Don't pretend you give a shit about your work.'

'Shut up. You're boring me.'

'My dad's really not doing very well.'

'Oh, okay. You can sit here with me a little while.'

'Thanks.'

I couldn't help it. When I came back to Bristol after the summer Richard died, I found myself looking forward to seeing Oliver. After that first night in Bristol when I'd slept with Luke, Oliver and I spent all our time together. I'd created a new safe space where the real world didn't exist and it was just us and a few others on the paper, focused on creating something new before the students had even got back for the term in September. The paper had always provided a focus and purpose to my student life, and as we were suspended between summer ending and term beginning, it was a wonderful distraction. As we plotted and worked on the paper intensely, I forgot any fears that soon the boys would be returning to the house and normal Bristol life for everyone else, but not for me, would begin. On one of those nights, Oliver and I had stayed up talking until sunrise and thought it'd be a fun idea to go and get a pint at a pub. We stopped on the way and sat on the wall outside someone's house for a cigarette. The conversation took a natural flow from talking about the paper, the students and mental health to Richard's suicide.

'What can we do?' Oliver asked.

'I don't know. We should really do something in the paper. Use our position. To do something.'

'Well, it's up to you, but I agree we should do something in the paper about it.'

There was a pause as we both had a drag on our cigarettes. I looked off into the distance and felt a pang of guilt. Oliver and the paper were a drug, a distraction that temporarily numbed the pain that Richard was gone. It was addictive, fun and thrilling to the point it felt like a betrayal.

'I don't know,' I said.

'It'd be good to talk about male suicide,' he said. I was in awe that he could speak those words out loud because I couldn't. For me, they felt so loaded with shame. I thought he looked so handsome and so sincere. He was wearing his red jacket. *Red was our colour.*

'Come then, let's go see what pubs are open, should we head this way?' I started walking off.

'Sure.'

'You're buying.' I turned back and smiled back at him.

'Haha, whatever.' He caught up with me.

Student deaths often made the front page of the newspaper. We'd take their profile picture off their Facebook page, so there'd be a grainy picture of them at the bottom of the front page, accompanied by a short piece about what they studied, their halls and how they died. No one mentioned covering Richard's death to me again and my shame about his death moved me further into avoidance; I let it slip past. But that conversation with Oliver that day on the wall meant everything to me because it would be the only one about Richard that I'd have at Bristol with someone who'd known us before he'd died. It was different from the conversation with Luke, which was more of a performance of my messiness to be intriguing to a male stranger. The conversation with Oliver was a precious and rare event where someone would look me in the eye and acknowledge that Richard had once been alive. But that was the extent of it. We never spoke of it again and we'd only really talked about it that time within the context of the paper.

The intense friendship with Oliver was short-lived as students returned to Bristol to start the term and classes began again. Oliver and I were no longer working on the paper every day and he started going out with the features editor of the paper, Amy. I'd work with her closely on the features pages and tried desperately to hide my irritation at how nice she was. There was a wide-eyed innocence to her and it prickled me that I'd been cast aside for a purer model.

The boys returned to the house and Richard was never spoken of. In second year, the boys had split into two groups where they'd cook for each other each night, but Richard and I would cook separately. Richard and I had isolated ourselves from the house in second year and I realised that that was partly why I was so scared of returning to the house with the boys. Dean invited me to join his cooking group with Fin and Jonny, which meant that I'd sit down and eat with them every day and so I felt more part of the house than I had in second year. We'd live off a rotation of fajitas, chicken curry, spaghetti bolognese and sausages and mash. It also meant that every four days I had something to do, which was to go to the Sainsbury's on Whiteladies Road to get ingredients to cook that night.

I was now in my third year of history and I had two hours of classes a week, therefore my weekend started at 1.30 p.m. on Monday. My days were filled with empty hours. I'd wake up as late as possible and I'd go and sit on Zac's bed and watch him play *Pro Evo*. Zac was a fellow history student, so, like me, was always in the house, whereas the rest of the boys studied science and so were out at lectures all day. Zac and I were two grieving people with nothing to do and so we spent a lot of time smoking on our doorstep.

White wine made me sad and I kept drinking it. There were days when I didn't want to leave my room, so I'd binge on boxsets, with the curtains and doors closed and the lights off. I watched *The O.C.*, I watched *24*, sometimes in 24 hours, placing the DVDs in my laptop and balancing it on the bed. This was my life of booze and boxsets in my small, dark room.

The student newspaper took up a few days of my time fortnightly. Having something to do was a relief and I transformed when I set foot inside the office. I had opinions and power and there was more to me than a dead boyfriend. I'd be surrounded by people, occupied with all the work we had to do and we'd always drink together when we were finished. I never wanted it to end, so I'd always be the last to leave and I'd walk home alone and drunk. When I got back, Zac was up. He was always up, with his door open, so I'd see him when I'd get back. He told me to stop walking home alone late at night and that there were six boys in the house who could always walk me home. I couldn't imagine asking any of them to do that. Our relationship seemed surface level, dominated by 'bants' and small talk. I shut the boys out from my grief and as I'd never spoken to any of them about what was happening with Richard in second year, I didn't talk to them about what was happening with me now. Asking for help would mean admitting to myself that I needed it, and it was easier to tell myself that I was okay if I was self-sufficient. I believed, with no evidence – just my shame talking – that no one in the house wanted to help carry the weight of my grief and that no one would have walked me home late at night, so I didn't ask.

Some weekends, I'd have a friend's twenty-first birthday party at another university. I'd go to every twenty-first I was invited to, spending money as if it could never run out, and I was always excited to escape Bristol and be with my home friends. As Richard was slipping away from me, I became increasingly obsessed with my own image. This is a habit I notice in myself today – as my self-esteem tumbles, my vanity rises. Richard had abandoned me, and the rejection from him and others because of the stigma surrounding my grief meant I felt unwanted, so I focused on my appearance, with the hope that an attractive exterior would make me more appealing to others. I put more make-up on, layering on my mask, believing it would hide the ugliness inside me. I looked in the mirror more, I took more photos of myself and I focused on how I looked a little too much. I went to people's twenty-first birthday parties and the act would begin: I'd drink too much, make a lot of noise, demand a lot of attention and take lots of photos of myself. My Facebook albums showed more and more pictures of my own face during this time. I had kept my slim grief-figure and I'd had a fringe cut that was a bit too short. I looked sharper and edgier than I had before and my image reflected the shield I'd built around myself, terrified anyone would see what was within.

There have been turning points in my life, and the day I walked into Zac's room in late October when Anna C. was visiting was one of them. Anna C. and I had spent ages getting ready to go out and even though my fringe was still a bit too short, I was looking good and wearing my scrabble necklace with a T on it. We walked into Zac's room and he caught my eye. He was holding his game console loosely in his hand and the turning point was when I noted that he took his eyes off *Pro Evo* for a bit too long.

Chapter 6

I Know What You Like

Anna S. told me that she could see it coming. She'd come up to Bristol for the weekend and we'd gone to a Halloween party dressed as cats. Years later, she admitted she knew what was going to happen between us.

'So, you could tell that he fancied me?'

'No, it was much more than that.'

I had sat very close, leaning on him at the kebab shop after the Halloween party.

It was November 2008 and 'Black and Gold' by Sam Sparro was blasting out of Zac's room. He'd been playing it loudly on repeat and I'd gone to stand in his doorway and seen him dancing about to it.

'I love this song,' I said.

'I know,' he said as he walked over to his laptop to turn it down.

'How do you know?'

'Because I know what you like.'

'Okay.'

'Plus, I can hear you playing your shit music through the walls.'

'Shut up.'

'You have a good singing voice by the way.'

I hesitated and looked at him. I'd always wanted to be a singer. How did he always know? In first year, when it was my birthday, the boys came back from a trip and Zac was sulking all night at the pub. I found out later that when they'd gone to buy me my present, they'd had a huge fight in HMV because he'd wanted to get me *Breakfast at Tiffany's* on DVD. He knew I hadn't seen it and they said I must have done because I had the poster on the back of my door. Zac had gone back and bought it and given it to me anyway, which was handy as he was right, I hadn't watched the movie.

I walked into his room and slumped myself on the edge of his bed. I thought of when he'd made fun of me in my earliest days of university for listening to The Smiths.

'What are you up to?'

'Nothing.'

'Cigarette?'

'Always.'

We both drank a lot and had nothing to do, and in my room late one night, we started kissing and couldn't stop. I was on top of him, humping him in my bed. I felt a fire inside me and I wanted to have sex with him. This was pure lust and I wasn't thinking about Richard in this moment – my guilt would come later when our relationship would develop to something more meaningful.

'No, let's wait,' he said.

'What, why?'

'Because I want to tell the boys about us first.'

'Why?'

'I'll talk to Dean first. Because it's the right thing to do.'

'Um, okay, I can't believe you're bringing up Dean right now. Like, who gives a fuck what he thinks?'

I wasn't thinking beyond that night and I had a strong desire to have sex with him. I sighed, 'Okay, I can't force you to have sex with me, but I'm so horny for you right now.'

'I am too.'

I fell asleep with my head resting on his chest. He woke up early, kissed me goodbye and sneaked next door back into his room before anyone else was up.

Having a body in my bed every night made it more bearable that Richard was dead. As I waited a few nights for Zac to talk to the boys one by one, we built up the sexual energy between us. I was finding him as good-looking as the night I'd met him. I felt waves of guilt as I'd lie there next to him, admiring his face when I'd suddenly think about Richard and what a betrayal this would be. I'd look forward or turn away as the guilt came over me. I felt as if I was cheating on Richard with his friend, even though they were never really friends and it can't be cheating if the person is dead. Richard had always said he didn't trust Zac and at my guiltiest moments, I wonder how he knew.

Then there was the fact that Zac was not to be taken too seriously. He often played the jester of the group. He had an argument with his girlfriend in first year and they ended up getting engaged, when that was not what he'd intended. They'd even gone to H. Samuel to get a ring. They eventually broke up, but still if anyone said sorry to anyone in our group, people would reply, 'Will you marry me?' and look at Zac at laugh. It was as though Zac was on a constant mission for people to underestimate him because he'd randomly disrupt his silliness with flashes of cutting insight and intelligence. He never did any work, yet effortlessly cruised through his exams and essays. He was deliberately complicated and yet he made me feel so simple when I was in his presence.

Merely days after our first kiss, I knew he'd talked to Dean because Dean came to my room and asked if I wanted to go to Sainsbury's with him. We walked there in silence for a bit. I knew what he was going to say, and he knew that I knew, but I thought I'd let him bring it up. I wasn't even sure where this was going to go. I wasn't sure what this Zac thing we were about to discuss even was. I saw it as a loophole that I had to get through before we could shag.

I deliberately engaged Dean in small talk as we left our house and walked towards the Whiteladies Road. Dean finally brought it up:

'Zac said that you guys were er…'

'Yeh.'

'I wanted to have a chat with you about it.'

We got to Sainsbury's and we kept going round and round the aisles. Dean was making fajitas, so he picked up the cheese, sour cream, chicken, peppers, onion and an Old El Paso kit. He'd pause in between talking whenever stood in front of an item, then he'd look at the prices, pick one up and continue.

'Why do we need to talk about it?' I said.

'Because, are you sure?'

'What do you mean?'

'I dunno, because it's *Zac*,' Dean said as he paused then picked up a packet of milk chocolate hobnobs.

'I don't like hobnobs.'

'Okay, well I do.'

'You could at least get biscuits I actually like considering I'm following you around fucking Sainsbury's.'

'Okay, which ones do you want?'

'Just the milk chocolate digestives.'

'Fine.' He put the hobnobs back and picked up the milk chocolate digestives. We went to the checkout and stood in the queue.

'Anyway, yeah so, Zac. Like it's *Zac*.'

'I don't know what you mean.' I did know what he meant. I'd surprised myself when I found myself drawn to him.

We paused as he completed the checkout and we walked back out to the Whiteladies Road.

'But you guys are like best friends,' I said.

'I know he's a best friend, but that doesn't mean you and him should er…'

'Why?' I asked. I wanted him to say it.

'Come on, you know why,' he stopped in the street and turned towards me and looked at me with a pained expression on his face.

'What do you want from me? I don't know what this thing is yet,' I said. 'He just wanted to speak to you all first. You don't have to watch over me all the fucking time.'

The eight of us gathered in the living room. Zac and I were sat on one of the red sofas which clashed horribly with the blue carpet. The rest of the boys were squished together on the sofa opposite us, perched on the sofa's arm, or were on our dining chairs. They were all facing us. It probably wasn't officially labelled a house meeting, but that's exactly what it looked and sounded like. I'd left a huge gap between me and Zac on the sofa and I was curled up leaning my head on the sofa's arm and he was sat on the other side in his Jack Wills navy tracksuit bottoms with his legs spread wide and his head resting in his hand and his elbow was upright on the sofa's arm.

I felt like a naughty school girl, but I also knew that Zac would get all the heat. It was because of Zac that Richard, Fin and I were in the house in the first place. He'd brought us in. Fin spent the whole time staring at the floor. The boys raised issues such as, what if it didn't work between us and it caused tension in the house? Zac assured the group that we'd talked about it, although I'm not sure if we had and he said we weren't suddenly going to become a two in the house. Zac was going to stay in his cooking group and I was going to stay in mine. Once we'd covered the obvious issues, an awkward silence descended over us.

'But, what about Richard?' Andy asked.

The question lingered as the word Richard hovered above us all in the room.

I lifted my head up and I smiled at Andy. I appreciated him saying Richard's name. There was silence as everyone suddenly turned towards me.

'Obviously, I've thought about that,' I said gently.

And that's all I had to say. I couldn't look at Zac, but I could see him reposition his leg out of the corner of my eye.

That was the first and the last time Richard's name was uttered in the house by the boys that year. I'd got used to not bringing him up or mentioning anything that had happened in first or second year involving Richard. I'd constantly edit memories and stories, leaving him out. Sometimes with Zac, I wanted to talk about Richard, but it was like a block and I just couldn't do it. I got the sense that Zac was angry with him for what he'd done and it made me uncomfortable, as I didn't want to admit that I was angry with Richard, too. But my anger wasn't enough to quell the guilt I felt for being with Zac.

It took me longer to surrender to the feelings of the relationship than Zac, who seemed to have decided that that's what he wanted it to be from day one, but, eventually, I was tumbling in love. He was reliable and loving and I felt safe around him. He was literally always there. We created a shell around us and a little life that existed within our two rooms that were next door to each other on our little corridor. I was no longer lonely and I was with someone who knew all my darkness. He knew about my dead boyfriend, the empty white wine bottles in my room and my terrible taste in music.

As I loved him more, I felt less guilty being with him and the sexual energy between us brought me back to life. We went on an adventurous sex escapade of trying new things in the middle of the day and there was a curiosity to it that engaged our bored history student minds. We'd have a lot of fun texting flirty sexy things to each other from our rooms next door when we were pretending to do some work. One day, he suggested we write each other letters about how much we loved each other.

The house quickly got used to our relationship and us as a couple. At home, it was as if we'd always been together and we only felt judgement on the rare occasion we'd grace the history department with our presence. We'd both managed to make enemies from our course –Luke's now ex-girlfriend knew about what had happened between me and him. I'm not sure how or why she knew, but the way her gaggle of girls who were the types who had always been popular at school would look over at me, I knew that she did. Then there was the girl who I'd been friendly with in second year, who had a thing with Zac that he'd ended abruptly and she called me straight after to tell me about it. Whenever she walked past us, she'd look straight ahead and storm past us, leaving a chill behind her. She deleted me on Facebook shortly after the news about me and Zac had got out, and I thought that was fair enough.

Richard and I had withdrawn from the group in second year, but Zac was more sociable with the boys and he brought me into the house. I felt more as if I had a family of brothers and I could sit with them in the living room or in Zac's room playing *Pro Evo*, and I felt happier going along to the pub with them when he was around. Something about the combined forces of the darkness we felt from our grief brought us both back into the light. We'd go into our rooms with each other at night rather than with a bottle of wine or whiskey. A calmness descended on the house as we all settled into our new way of being with each other. My relationship with Zac moved very quickly as we were together all day, every day, and so within six weeks we'd formed the foundations of a solid relationship.

By the Christmas holidays, Zac was back home with me and my friends at The Old White Lion Pub, the pub where I'd spent my whole summer grieving Richard. The fire and passion of the relationship brought with it some challenges and they were further pronounced when we were removed from the safety of our rooms, our corridor and our home on Ashgrove Road in Bristol. My home friends seemed suspicious of him, too, which unsettled us both. It lit the match to set fire to my guilt and it similarly made Zac feel rejected. This also meant my home friends were more witness to the tumultuous side of the relationship rather than the calm day to day we had at Bristol. They also weren't witness to the person I'd been in term-time before I'd started my relationship with Zac. They never saw me bingeing on boxsets and drinking alone in my dingy room in Bristol.

Zac was a person who sulked. He'd sulk if Manchester United lost the football, he'd sulk if he was disappointed that a plan had changed, he'd sulk if he thought I was ignoring him. At our first New Year's Eve party together, we were at my friend Rosie's dad's house and Zac just walked out. I left and chased him down the empty streets of St John's Wood. He said I'd been ignoring him all night as I clearly didn't want him there and I just wanted to talk to my friends. I hurried to keep up with him, switching between my own embarrassment-fuelled anger and wanting to reassure him and make it okay again. The truth was, I didn't need him as much when I was here in London as when I was in Bristol where I'd hide behind him. We didn't know how to be together in the outside world.

The arguments were exhausting. They'd go on and on and around and around in circles. They're the thing I remember most vividly about the relationship. I can still feel the desperation in me as I'd beg him to stop sulking. It took days for him to come out of the stupor when I got back from visiting Anna C. in Durham for her twenty-first in January. I spent part of Anna S.'s twenty-first talking to him on the phone because he was upset that I hadn't texted him back. I finally cracked when I was working at Koko in Camden in London and he got angry that I hadn't replied to him while I was on my shift. I didn't reassure him that time. He apologised and acknowledged that was wrong. He was also the most jealous boyfriend I had, which I put down to him previously not being the best-behaved boyfriend himself. Funnily enough, despite knowing this about his past, I trusted him completely.

I wasn't innocent. The anger in me that had moved in during the summer was still so strong. I threw a water bottle at him and it hit his head once. I'd crossed a line when that happened and I stood there staring back at him. We went for a cigarette and he explained to me that it couldn't happen again. It didn't. I'd scared myself and I felt so ashamed for what I'd done.

We were united in our grief and yet we could barely speak of it because we felt our own pain was of greater magnitude than the other person's. Neither of us could compute how the other one had suffered more than the other. I'd lost my first love, the person I was with all day, every day. He'd lost his father, the man who'd been there his whole life.

And so, while things could be bad between us, I can still remember how it felt to be so wholly seen and understood. He just knew me inside out and sometimes showed he knew me better than I knew myself; at times it was as if he could articulate my thoughts or predict my behaviour or response to something before I could. I also knew he knew all the things about me that I didn't like about myself and yet he still wanted me. He had seen me avoid and ignore Richard's depressive decline and all the shame I held on to and the blame I put on myself for causing Richard's death. Sometimes I'd put so much blame on myself that my mind would tell me I was akin to a murderer, and yet still, Zac loved me and was always by my side. And so, although the scenes in my mind, even after all this time, flit between our endless arguments, fights, sulks and sex, I can't forget how it felt to be so seen and to connect so deeply with someone. I'd never experience that again and I became riddled with regret with what would happen between us. It'd add another layer of torture to my broken heart.

But while we were in our third year of university and Zac and I were together, my life was a lot better with him in it. It felt more bearable to be alive and my days felt that they had a point to them. We both drank less, socialised more and even occasionally did some work. But there was still a destructive, chaotic and volatile streak bubbling inside me. I seemed particularly angry at my history studies. I'd bash out random words on the page and often didn't read essays before handing them in. After Richard died, I was given extendable submission deadlines and I'd always try to get them in for the date, but I'd then find it impossible to meet the deadline when I didn't have to.

I gave no thought to what was coming after university. I felt as if my university experience had been robbed from me. For my dissertation, I just sat down for a few days to get to the word count. I'd go to the British Library, aimlessly flick through books and hang out with friends on breaks. I just wanted to hand it in on the deadline and not think about it. Zac took the pages of my dissertation off me as I was about to hand it in and he started reading it.

'You can't hand this in,' he said.

'Why not?'

'It doesn't make any sense. You've just put sentences all over the place.'

'I don't care.'

'You can't hand this in. Email your tutor now and get an extension and we'll do it together.'

'Fine.'

I shot out an email to my tutor asking for a deadline extension. Zac handed his in. I wasn't sure when he'd got his done. Straight after handing his in, he sat at the computer in his room and I sat on his bed and we went through my dissertation, line by line, changing the words on the page so they made sense.

The student newspaper had lost its sheen for me and I ended up recklessly quitting it before the end of the year. I found being around Oliver confusing and I was still resentful that he'd been made editor and not me. We had occasional moments of conversational chemistry, but not enough to stop me feeling distant from him, and Luke was an annoying reminder of my time at Bristol before I'd found Zac. The paper wasn't really a place I could escape to anymore, but another stressful place full of people who didn't know or care about what had happened to me. There was one night in second year when Richard had come out with Oliver, me and two of the other editors and there was a picture of all of us. Oliver asked who'd taken the picture and it stung me that he'd forgotten. He would later contact me to tell me we'd won a *Guardian* Student Media Award.

I wanted to make my world as small and as safe as possible. I wanted to stay in that life of third year, going to Sainsbury's on Whiteladies Road, watching DVDs on my laptop in my room or sitting on Zac's bed while the boys played *Pro Evo*. I wanted to stay forever eating chicken fajitas or bolognese at home with the boys and continue to live in our mundane routine. But as life had become more bearable for me, tragedy struck our house again.

Chapter 7

Whom the Gods Love Die Young

I can still hear the sound of his mother's scream when she found him dead.

That day had been like any other, the main activity had been that Zac and I had gone to Sainsbury's together because it was his turn to cook for his cooking group and I had to get food because it was Fin's turn to cook in my group, but he'd been in his room all day because he was ill. I complained how annoying it was that Fin wasn't making dinner. I bought some chicken goujons and a mint-chocolate Viennetta because it was on offer.

Shortly after Zac and I got back, Fin's mother and brother knocked on the door saying they wanted to check up on Fin as they hadn't heard from him all day and he usually called them every day. His mother and brother lived in Blagdon, which was a village near Bristol. We let them in and I went back in my room as they went into Fin's room, and then I heard the scream.

'What's happening?' I asked.

'He's dead.' Zac was pale, his eyes were wide and his hands moved from his chest towards the floor, as he said the word dead.

'What do you mean?' You don't think people mean that when they say that.

'Dead.'

I walked past Zac and into Fin's room and saw Fin on the floor, topless, the colour drained from his body and his lips. Dean was leaning over him, pumping his chest and breathing into his mouth. My heart started racing and I walked straight out again.

We gathered outside the flat once the ambulance arrived. We stood, leaning against the steps that led to our front door. Dean was inside with the paramedics.

'Is Dean okay?' I asked Andy, who had been in the room with him while he was trying to resuscitate him. My mouth had said those words to fill the silence.

'No, of course he's not alright,' Andy snapped back.

A prickly sensation rushed through my body and I felt very self-conscious standing there next to him. I moved away from them all and called my mum.

'Hello,'

'What's happened?' she said.

'It's Fin. He... he.'

The paramedics came out and told us that he wouldn't be going in their ambulance and we'd have to wait for some sort of special death ambulance to take him away. We went back inside and sat around the dining room table and waited in silence.

'Evi and Daneal said we can go round to theirs,' one of the boys said.

No one replied.

We then saw the stretcher roll past the door, carrying Fin's body which was covered from head to toe with a blanket with straps around it. And just like that, Fin was gone.

His heart had stopped in the night. He'd been lying there dead in his room all day.

Zac's mother arranged for Zac and me to stay at a hotel in the Bristol City Centre. We packed a bag and jumped into a cab while the rest of the boys started walking to Evi and Daneal's house. We checked into our room and went down to the hotel bar and drank whiskey, mumbling on repeat how we couldn't believe this could have happened, getting more philosophical about life and death as we poured the whiskey down our throats. I never said what I was really thinking. How could this be the second death in a year. How?

We went back to our room, sat drinking more whiskey on the sofa and I was terrified of what would come next. Zac was tired, he said. So, although I was scared to go to sleep, we went to bed. I lay there awake all night, making sure I could still hear him breathing. If I fell asleep, I'd jolt awake. I couldn't let him die in the night, too. I couldn't admit to him the next morning that that was the real reason I'd lain awake all night.

The next day, Zac and I went back to the house and back to our corridor we'd shared with Fin on the top floor. It was the summer term before our final exams, so we didn't have much longer in the house. Fin's door was open and we could see all his stuff in it and his bedsheets all in chaos. Zac walked down the corridor and closed the door to Fin's room.

Whom the gods love die young. We all die and for some of us it happens sooner than for others. It always seems that the ones who are taken from us too soon are better than the ones who are left behind. There are so many clichés we say when people die: the impact they had on those around them, their far-reaching potential, how they were full of life or bursting with joy. Perhaps those words are said for comfort, but there's no one for whom these clichés are truer than Fin. He laughed the most, he was the kindest, he was certainly going to be the most successful because he was already doing more with his life than the rest of us. He was taken from us too soon. And he had no choice in the matter, he didn't want his time to be up. And so, with Fin, it was how – how can you just die in the night? How can your heart just stop? How can life just be snatched from you in an instant like that? How can something so big be so completely outside our control? I didn't know you could just die like that. *Unlike suicide, this means that we can all just die.* We were suddenly confronted with our mortality, and at 20 years old, I wasn't ready for that lesson yet.

I first heard of Fin in Yia Mass bar on the second night of
Freshers' Week and I was told there was a boy from Blagdon
whom Richard had befriended who'd never had alcohol before,
or maybe it was just that he'd never tried shots – either way I
remember thinking it was deeply controversial. That's insane, I said
to whoever had told it to me. It was possibly the most scandalous
thing I'd heard about anybody during Freshers' Week and I was
fascinated. While Fin adjusted to the constant downing of shots
during Freshers' Week, he never quite lost that innocence to him.
It was an innocence that gave him a genuine enthusiasm for what
seemed like everything. He lacked the cynicism and meanness that
was so often central to the ability of any university student to make
any joke. As with Richard, it's Fin's laugh that comes back to me
so vividly. He was always wearing his yellow hoodie, which was,
like him, unapologetically bright. Fin was a talented photographer
and his photos brought some class to our otherwise grainy, terrible
and drunken photo albums on our Facebook pages.

Fin and I had grown apart in third year. He was Richard's best
friend and perhaps without that connection there, we weren't
physically as much in the same room. Perhaps we'd both become
withdrawn in our grief. He'd lost his father that summer, and
Richard and he had been very good friends. We'd been a three,
we'd come into the house together, and yet we never spoke about
the one missing from our trio. In first year, I'd meet them both
after their computer science lectures and we'd head to Boulangerie
on Park Street and eat baguettes. There are so many pictures on
Facebook of the three of us hanging out in first year and I'm so
grateful that we existed in an era where it was normal to upload
a bunch of photos of us doing nothing together in my Goldney
Hall bedroom. Those ordinary but precious moments are forever
captured and I now look at them often.

Fin was a big character on Bristol's gay scene. When he died, a
group that called themselves 'The Gays' gathered at the university

campus and streets of Woodland Road and went around telling people in person that Fin was dead, trying to reach them before they saw it on Facebook. Before Fin had gone to bed for the last time, he'd updated his Facebook status saying that he felt really sick and uncomfortable that night.

There was an outpouring of grief on Fin's Facebook wall that didn't happen on Richard's Facebook page and it pained me to see it. People still write on Fin's wall to this day. The tone of everything that happened after Fin's death was so different from Richard's suicide death. A nasty, visceral feeling of jealousy stirred up in me when I saw the difference in how people were reacting to Fin's death in comparison to Richard's. I felt shame for even having such ugly thoughts and emotions as my own response to Fin's death, but I couldn't help it. I craved that same level of outpouring of grief for Richard that Fin was getting. There was a simplicity and an innocence to the response to Fin's death that didn't exist for Richard and I didn't know if it was because Richard had died by suicide or if it was something else, but I couldn't help but feel sad about the difference that was unfolding in front of me.

We were told to not wear black at the funeral, which was packed. I stood together with the boys from the house in a group, now forever bound by tragedy. I was next to Zac and holding on to him the whole time. The humanist funeral service talked about Fin's death in what I thought was a shockingly matter-of-fact way. It talked about how he'd died in a natural way and how it just was. When they referred to the natural causes of his death, I couldn't help but think how un-natural the cause of Richard's death had been. I also thought how unfair it was that someone who'd wanted to keep living had been robbed by nature of the chance to do so.

The wake was at a bar in Blagdon with a huge outdoor space that overlooked beautiful Blagdon Lake. The drinks were flowing and we relaxed into it as we knocked the gin and tonics and vodka-sodas back. I sat on Zac's lap and we were almost having fun, drunk and laughing together. Once it was over, a group of us went to Pizza Express in Clifton. This was something we were all in together. I thought of Richard's funeral and how his friends turned away from me. The contrast made me wince as I looked down at my La Reine pizza.

It was May 2009, Fin was dead and our final year exams weren't far away. Second-year exams counted for 50 per cent and third year another 50 per cent, including the dissertation, which thanks to Zac, I'd managed to get a decent 2:1 grade for. I'd also done fairly well in second year. Shortly after Fin had died, Zac and I went to the history department to have a meeting about our exams in light of the tragedy we'd experienced that year. We kept getting lost as we tried to find the main office as we frequented the history department so irregularly. All I recall from the meeting is when the woman said to Zac, 'We feel especially sorry for you,' it angered me that his father's death was considered worse than the grief I was feeling for Richard. It wasn't a hierarchy, but her comments made me feel that way and if ever I felt as if someone was implying that my response to Richard's death was out of proportion, it hit a nerve. I felt a certain stigma about how awful I'd felt when he'd died when we hadn't even known each other for two years.

I did my final exams and got my 2:1. We made it to the end of our final year in Bristol. I graduated, wearing the black shoes I'd bought for Richard's funeral on my graduation day. I'd made it to the end of university, but the past year had changed me forever, and not necessarily for the better.

Part Two

Escaping

Chapter 8

Option C

I was sitting in the driver's seat of my mum's car, parked around the corner from the job centre in Finchley Central. I checked the time on my phone and I had a few minutes to spare. I picked up the pieces of paper which were lying on the front seat next to me and I reached down to pull out a pen from my handbag on the floor. I pushed the paper against the steering wheel, pulled the pen lid off with my mouth and started filling in the section of the form where you had to write the five jobs you'd applied for in the past two weeks. I tried to remember the few random places I'd sent applications off to. In the past two weeks, I'd been for one job interview at a yoghurt company. My first job had been selling newspapers, I'd sold clothes at Joy in Bristol, I'd been an estate agent the summer after first year in Bristol and I'd had a job in telesales when Richard had died. I wrote some sales jobs down. I slightly resented that my path seemed to be heading for sales because I'd felt sales had chosen me rather than I'd chosen it. Yet I did nothing about it as two weeks would fly by and I'd find myself back in the car, filling out the same form and trying to recall which jobs I'd applied for in that time.

I cringed thinking about the job interview I'd had at the yoghurt company.

'I get the sense you don't want this job,' my interviewer, a middle-aged white man with grey hair, had said.

I looked back at him, allowing for enough hesitation in my response to confirm he was right. The interview had got off to an awkward start. The job, as far as I understood it, was to drive around, visiting supermarkets and discussing with store managers where the yoghurts were going to be placed in the store, as positioning of items makes a huge difference to sales in supermarkets. I'd taken my mother's car for the interview and driven outside London to a retail space off the motorway. As I sat down in a dingy room with no windows, the yoghurt man asked:

'What car do you have?'

'Oh I don't know, maybe like a Citroen.'

'Which model?'

'Um, I don't know.'

'You don't know what car you have?' he said.

'I don't, no.'

'Okay…'

'So what do you know about this job?'

'Um…'

The thought of driving around the country and looking at yoghurt in supermarkets didn't appeal to me at all, but then again nothing was appealing to me.

The job-centre people didn't seem too concerned about me and they didn't enquire too much about my job-seeking – I suspect because I came across as polished – so I was in and out of there in ten minutes. The main challenge of my fortnightly interviews was to turn up on time, which I managed to struggle with. They'd sign me off, and off I'd go, guaranteeing my £47.95 per week, which, without appreciating how fortunate I was to be living at home for free, I mostly spent on booze and fags.

My days were spent in my childhood bedroom on my laptop, browsing random job websites and looking for anything that I could apply for. So many of my friends were also at a loss for what to do about their work. There was a general malaise in the air about graduating in the aftermath of the recession. It felt as if we were looking for work during an era of broken promises and it turned out that real life had been a disappointment for so many of us.

Finally, I got myself a six-week internship at a company that described itself as a startup. It was also my first experience of doing PR. The company was a graduate recruitment website and they desperately wanted to get into student newspapers. I knew that the greatest challenge of a student newspaper editor is to find anything at all to write about. I called some student newspaper editors, landed some coverage for the startup and was lauded a hero.

I enjoyed working there, but the six weeks were coming to an end and although there was a chance that that time would be extended, I didn't want to risk it. Zac got me a job through a contact of his mum at a TV post-production company. My job was to invite people to the Christmas party and to ask what they were working on to see if there was an opportunity to sell the company's post-production services. I was grateful for the job at first and it was pleasant enough, but I soon felt horrifically lonely. The graduate recruitment startup had a couple of other interns so I had peers to talk to in the day, but here I was an isolated unit. The other young people were all runners who were there with the plan to do their time serving senior post-production people and work their way up to a production job one day. They were in the TV industry for the long term, whereas I wasn't and I hated how the people my age who I desperately wanted to chat to would only talk to me to come and ask what I wanted for lunch that day. If I went outside for a cigarette and any of them were outside too, they'd ignore me and so, after some hesitation, I'd sit on a different bench, alone and thinking how excruciatingly far away 6 p.m. felt.

After Christmas, there was no more party and therefore no more job to do, and so I was back in my childhood bedroom on GChat all day. Zac and I had enjoyed a drama-free New Year's Eve and the dynamic of me without a job and him in an admin role and talking to me all day suited us well. We were very happy going back and forth between our parents' respective London houses. We didn't realise that our lives were hanging in the balance between university and the real world and we didn't know that something was coming that was going to throw a hand grenade into our peaceful, although somewhat meaningless, lives.

There was a buzz on Facebook. In what *The Sunday Times* would describe as 'a cross between *Big Brother* and *The Apprentice*', the advertising agency Saatchi & Saatchi launched a competition where you were to make a Facebook group and amass the highest number of members in weeks. The prize was that you got through to the second round of challenges for its internship, eventually earning a place on one of its ten unpaid six-week placements. There were four jobs available after the internship. I had little interest or knowledge of the advertising industry, but everyone was doing it and so I thought I would too. I started my group and called it Secret London. My thinking was that people could share the secrets of the city and cool clubs, bars and restaurants to go to. I thought the group would feed our desire to both be in the know and be able to show we know where to go. I thought the word 'secret' would lure people in further and I thought it would be helpful as I quite wanted to know where to go in London, too.

I set up the Facebook group, stole a tube picture off a Google Images search and went out for the day. As I was standing on the platform in Kings Cross, waiting to switch onto the Hammersmith and City line, I got a text from Anna S.

Anna S.: *Have you seen your group? It has thousands already xx*

Me: *OMG no xx*

It grew and it grew. It got to 180,000 in two weeks. I was suddenly a mini-celebrity on Facebook. Everyone was talking to me about it. People were saying how amazing it was that my group was growing so fast.

Secret London was popping with people talking about where to go for anything you could think of. As the group grew and grew, the excitement of others rubbed off on me and it was as if the internet had given me a purpose and direction. I wanted to seize this opportunity and so I decided I wanted to turn Secret London into a business, but I had no idea what that meant. I knew no business people to ask and no part of my schooling had prepared me for it either.

At the British Library, Humanities Two had been the room where I'd bashed out my incoherent dissertation, but for this project, I went to sit in the Business Centre for the first time. A lot of my friends were still studying and so I had people to eat lunch with. I told them I wanted to turn Secret London into a business; even though I didn't know how, I just knew I wanted to do it. Secret London had given me a new energy. I felt shiny again. I was no longer defined by my boyfriend who had killed himself, but by something I'd created. I flicked through some business books and I had no understanding of what I was reading or what I should do next, but there was a drive in me that wanted to find out.

Zac suggested I started a Twitter account for Secret London.

'I don't get Twitter, there's no photos. Is it just like a boring Facebook?'

'It's going to be huge.'

'Fine, fine.'

I set a Twitter up for myself and one for Secret London, and in February 2010 I posted my first-ever tweet.

Not long afterwards, I got a call from Anthony, with whom I'd worked at the graduate recruitment startup. He was the one who had interviewed me and I suspect fought for me to get the job. I'd had a dramatic incident a couple of days before my interview at the graduate recruitment startup where some insect bites on my legs had got infected and one of my legs had swelled to a balloon. Anna C. had driven me to Finchley Memorial Hospital to get it checked out and I was spacey and tired during my interview from the swelling and itching, and the antihistamine and antibiotics I was on. Anthony, who everyone called Tony, later said that his instinct was right that something was up in the interview and he was glad that he'd given me a chance.

Tony called me to say a temping agency had got in touch with him for a reference and he was wondering what I was up to now because he was working at a new hospitality startup. I told him about Secret London.

We arranged to meet near their offices around Oxford Circus and I called him when I got out of the tube station. He told me to meet him at Caffè Nero on Regent Street. I went into Caffè Nero, ordered a cappuccino and went to sit at a table upstairs with my coffee. Moments later, Tony came up the stairs, followed by a man of about 30 and another man my age. The three of them took seats surrounding me on the table and introduced themselves. My coffee was still too hot to drink.

'I thought we'd go for lunch.' The one who was 30 said.

'Oh, sorry, I didn't realise… I just got this coffee.'

'You can finish it.'

'Um, okay.'

I sat there awkwardly as they watched me and I tried to sip a coffee that was too hot as fast as I possibly could, burning the roof of my mouth.

'I thought we'd go to Strada?' The man in his thirties said.

'Okay,' I said, still taken aback by my misunderstanding of the setting of this meeting.

As I sat at the table at Strada, the pizza restaurant that in 2010 was considered one notch above Pizza Express, I tried to concentrate on what the men were saying to me while wondering what I should order. I also started to panic about how this worked. Do I offer to pay? Do I just let them pay? I browsed the pizza menu and tried to work out what might be easiest to eat. I wanted the pepperoni pizza, but then I feared that could be an unsophisticated thing to order.

After lunch, they suggested we go back to their offices on Hanover Square. I was tired from the overwhelming intensity of lunch: they'd talked fast and I was unsettled but didn't know how to say no, so I agreed. Once we were back in the very, very small room which had a whiteboard on the wall behind one of their desks, I pulled up a chair and sat there, mostly in silence as one of the men started enthusiastically drawing on the whiteboard what a website for Secret London could look like. He was very high energy and he kept drawing and drawing and rubbing out on the whiteboard. I'd never seen anything or anyone like it and in my overwhelmed state I struggled to focus on what he was saying; but when it came to an end and I left their office, I felt a twinge of excitement. I knew that a big change was coming even though I didn't quite understand what.

As I got back out to the dark streets of Hanover Square, I took out my phone and saw Zac had sent me a few texts asking if I was okay. I called him and with each sound of the phone ringing and step I took towards the station, I felt increasingly excited about what this meeting might mean for Secret London.

'Hey.'

'Hi,' he said in the low, sad voice he used when he was upset with me.

'How are you?'

'Not good. I was worried. You were offline for five hours.'

'Okay, sorry, I know. I went back to their offices and we were drawing out all these plans for Secret London and I couldn't get out my phone and lost track of time.'

'Well, I was worried.'

'Okay, sorry, but I'm fine. It was really exciting. We mapped out what the website could be and stuff. And these guys are like experienced founders who get business.'

'You sound enthusiastic,' the deadpan of his tone contrasted with the energy of mine.

'Why can't you be happy for me?'

'Because I'm not sure if I trust these guys.'

'You don't even know them. Anyway, I'm almost at the station now.

'Be careful.'

'What the fuck does that even mean?

'I'm just telling you to be careful.'

'Urgh, okay, I have to go now, bye.'

I got on the tube at Oxford Circus to go back home. I slumped onto my seat on the train. I was physically exhausted, but my mind was buzzing. Could this be it? After the year from hell, had I been sent something that would save me?

Tony rang me the next day and laid out some options for me for how we may want to proceed.

'Tiff. We have three options… Option A) You keep going with your own site build and we stay in touch. B) You come and work alongside us at our office. C) We help you build the website, put some money into it and it goes under our hospitality startup.'

I emailed him back the following day:

Hi Anthony,

I've given it some thought over the weekend and think I would be happiest if we went ahead with option c (going ahead with building the website) and finding a way for it to work for your startup. Thought best to email as it's a Sunday! If you want

*to chat, I'm available and on my phone all day. I also check
my emails regularly.*

*Best wishes,
Tiffany*

Years later, Tony would be talking about whenever he gave an offer
to someone, he would give them three options and they're meant to
go for option B. 'You're always meant to go for option B,' he said.

I was impatient and scared to seek advice from anyone in case
they changed my mind. I was desperate to shed my skin and start
afresh, so I went for option C: *I think I would be happiest if we
went ahead with option C.*

'I knew you'd call me today,' Zac said.

It was Saturday and I'd spent my first week in the little EasyJet
office on Hanover Square working alongside the founders. Zac
and I hadn't spoken for days after we argued about my decision to
go for option C. Shortly after I'd made my decision, I'd gone into
the office to sign some papers and once that was done, the founder
said, 'Our first employee. We should celebrate!'

News that I was going to be building a site was published on the
tech website, *TechCrunch*, which led to a huge amount of attention.
We were preparing for a Valentine's weekend where we'd build the
site with a large group of volunteers. The main two founders were
mostly out of the office and so I'd be alone with the younger one
or a designer they arranged for me to work with. On the Saturday
after my first week with them, I was ready to deal with Zac.

'You can't just toss me to one side when something exciting
comes along.'

'I'm not doing that, Zac. I've just not had a spare moment this
week and I want you to be supportive.'

'I've had the week from hell. I've left Facebook as it's "Tiffany Land" at the moment.'

'That's not really my fault.'

'No, I've had enough.'

He'd done this a few times before and I just thought I was calling his bluff. And then what I said next would turn out to be something I'd always regret, 'Okay. FINE. I'm sick of your shit anyway.'

I hung up the phone and I hung up the tragedy of the previous year with it. I was done with being the victim of my grief and that meant leaving Zac behind. It was time for me to dance off into a new world and I wanted others to see me as a successful entrepreneur. Zac was right, Facebook was Tiffany Land and I enjoyed it. I kept checking my emails and Facebook and watched as the group continued to grow and the attention was all on me. The rush, as so many people emailed me and Facebooked me, was somehow quietening. The prestige of being featured in *TechCrunch* meant that within weeks I'd gone from a person who'd felt so isolated in their grief it was as if I was infectious, to someone people were impressed by and wanted to be close to. What had started giving me a purpose became a source of external validation that I hadn't realised I'd so desperately been craving. If I went to a party, an acquaintance would proudly introduce me as 'The Secret London Girl'. I fed off the attention so much that it became easy to push thoughts of Zac to one side. I was numb to the fact that we'd broken up; a denial so deep that I wasn't aware of it. While I loved him and he'd brought me so much comfort, he'd always be associated with a person I didn't want to be from a time I didn't want to go back to. I wanted to be new and to bury the gnarly feeling of brokenness that lived inside of me. The more admired I was by others, the further I could hide my cracks from them and myself.

I embarked on the Secret London website build. The founders would later joke that it was the best recruitment event they'd ever done. They found an empty garage space which was part of an office complex on Bowling Green Lane in Clerkenwell. We were joined by an army of volunteers for the Secret London website-build weekend. Some of the volunteers had worked with me on the student newspaper, others were interested in startups or already knew the founders, and a few were random people who'd heard about it and wanted to give up their time to support it. There was one volunteer who briefly caught my attention when he arrived. He was tall, with bright, sharp blue eyes, a strong jaw and floppy brown hair. He was wearing a duffel coat which didn't fit him well.

'There's some space for you to sit over there.' I pointed him in the direction of the table I wasn't sitting on.

After a while, he came over to say that he was leaving.

'Oh, Francis. That's a shame.'

'It's Valentine's weekend.'

'So?'

'I've got a date.'

'Dating is what Americans do. We don't do that here in England. We get drunk, shag and then just go out.' I looked him in the eye.

'Ha, okay, anyway, I've got to go.'

There was a party atmosphere that weekend as we stayed late into the evenings. I was running on adrenaline and there was a purposeful fun to it that you only get when people gather to create something new. Startup culture suited me and I told *The Sunday Times* that I was 'doing to *Time Out* what *Wikipedia* did to the *Encyclopaedia Britannica*'. This was the sort of grandiose statement I'd so frequently hear in startup land in the years that were to come. I went on *Sky News*, I was featured in *The Sunday Times*, the *Evening Standard* and my local paper. It was sobering when Richard's parents emailed me to say they'd seen my article in *The Sunday Times*. It reminded me of the sadness that I was holding on to and of the person I didn't want to be anymore that this Secret London venture was helping me escape. Perhaps I saw their email as warning that I could never fully shed my past, no matter how hard I tried. I paused for a moment after I read their email, thanked them and went back to the energy of the room.

Once the weekend was over and the silence had settled over the office, what felt like an eternity had only been a few days. Zac got in touch to suggest we meet up in Farringdon in the middle of the week to give each other our stuff back. I asked if I could keep his navy cashmere jumper which I loved so much. He had a new one and this one had holes in it, but I still wore it all the time. It was the softest jumper I'd ever owned and brought me comfort, and I'd never admitted this, but I didn't want to let it go as it held memories of happier times between us and all the good and warmth he'd brought me. He said no. I also wanted to keep the *Mad Men* DVDs my mum had given him for Christmas because he didn't want to watch the show and I did. He said no, again. I thought he was being unreasonable and Dean got in touch with me to tell me to give everything Zac had asked for back. So, I conceded and packed it all into a bag, smelling and hugging that jumper for one last time, and took it to the office with me. At lunchtime, I told the founders I had to go and meet my ex-boyfriend to give him some of his things back. They looked over at the big bag of stuff next to me. 'Yes, personal life is important,' the founder said.

Zac and I met at the station and sat in the garden of a horrifically corporate restaurant in Farringdon. It was February and we were the only ones sat outside, looking into the main restaurant which was full of business men in suits. I started crying after our drinks arrived. Zac didn't reach out to comfort me. I kept crying and it all tumbled out of me. I talked about how overwhelmed I was, how scared I was of this monster that I'd created that had spun out of control, how I didn't know what was going to happen next, how I was tied to these founder men who I didn't really know. How I was sick of being 'The Secret London Girl', how hollow the feeling was of everyone wanting a piece of me just because of this thing I didn't even intend to create.

'Well, that's the decision you made,' he said.

There was silence as that statement hovered over us. The person who'd always been there for me, wasn't there for me anymore. We finished our drinks and parted ways. His half-hug crushed me. As I walked back to the office, my teary eyes began to glaze over and I picked up the pace and started walking with a new determination to give myself over to this new world that was waiting for me in the garage of Bowling Green Lane. I no longer wanted to be the terrified girl crying to Zac, who'd been cold to me; I was walking back to find warmth in being The Secret London Girl.

Chapter 9

I Hate You

'TP, are you coming?'

'Yeah, just give me one sec.' I had stopped on Whitechapel High Street and my flatmates had gone ahead and turned back to call after me. I had the payment terminal in one hand and my neck bent to my right side, holding the phone between my ear and my shoulder as I slowly walked down Whitechapel High Street, taking payment details from a customer for the hospitality startup. It was February 2011, one year after I'd signed the contract and one year after the Secret London site-build weekend.

I finished punching the credit card details of the person on the other end of the phone into the terminal, pressed enter, tore the receipt off the top and placed the payment terminal in my handbag. Then I ran to catch up with Daneal and Evi. I was now doing bookings, which meant I'd wake up to booking requests from Australia and fall asleep to emails from America. I was on my emails all the time and I carried that payment terminal with me everywhere, so I was always ready to take bookings. I took it to the pub, to Sainsbury's, to people's birthdays, and would often lie sleeping with it beside my bed.

'You and that machine. It's not normal,' Daneal said.

'I know, I know.'

Not long after the Secret London weekend, we got the news that Facebook groups were changing to company pages and soon we'd be losing all the members from the group, and therefore we'd be losing the thing that made the group valuable. This was devastating news as it meant that all our work would have been for nothing. We then saw that you could create events connected to Facebook groups and I presumed this meant you could instantly invite everyone on the Facebook group to an event and so that could be a way to transfer everyone over to the new 'page' format. I then shifted focus on creating an in-person Secret London event and I got in touch with the people who organised the festival Secret Garden Party. I couldn't believe it when I heard back from them and went for a meeting with them – everyone knew they put on the best events at the time. During my meeting, the Secret Garden Party people wrote down the name of the hospitality startup, when I mentioned they were connected to Secret London. The woman kept drawing a circle around the name of the startup as we spoke for the rest of the meeting. I bounced out of the meeting as I was excited that they were even considering collaborating on a Secret London event. When I got back to the office, I sat at my desk next to the founder, who was hunched over and staring at his screen. Without looking up at me, he said:

'Are you sure you can invite everyone on your group page automatically to an event?' His eyes flicked to the side in my direction.

'Yeah, I think so.'

'Are you sure?' I could tell he was reading something on the screen.

'Um, I think so,' I said again. It was at that moment that I realised that I wasn't sure at all. I'd just wanted it to be true. He got up and walked over to stand next to me.

'You can't. That's not how it works.'

There was silence as we both absorbed what this meant. The whole thing would crumble to ashes.

'Open an Excel Sheet.'

'Okay.' I opened Excel as he stood over me.

'Okay, so if these are the columns and this is your budget, how would you divide that up for Secret London moving forward?'

I stared at the screen and the squares were confusing me. I didn't know the answer. I got up and went to the loo and cried. When I came back, he said to me, 'You know, you shut down when you're stressed.'

Despite everyone trying to pull strings at Facebook, the Secret London group switched to a page and all the hundreds of thousands of members evaporated. Some members re-joined, the site limped along and one of the founders drew a triangle of price, time and quality and would say that we went for cheap and fast and that's why the quality of the site suffered. The Twitter account, which had been Zac's idea, continued to grow and thrive and I kept managing it just for my own pleasure. I'd retweet requests from people, such as where to go or what to do in London, and people would always swiftly reply with their recommendations. I loved having the tool myself when I was out late in an area and wanted to know where was still open at this time. I only ever had to wait moments for an answer.

The founders said that they had to go back to focusing on building their business, or 'our company' they'd say to me, correcting me if I ever said 'your company'. As part of my transition, Tony took me to buy an iPhone to replace my Motorola burgundy flip phone, which had always run out of space for text messages. Nobody I knew had an iPhone yet and I thought it was cool because it had Facebook on it. My shiny new smartphone would soon turn into a portable prison, with a continuous stream of work emails.

At the end of January 2011, after one year of working at the hospitality startup, they gave me a pay rise from £16k a year to £23.5k and told me that it was 'so you can move out of home'. I moved out immediately and into a flat with Evi and Daneal and another friend of theirs who was also from Bristol, on an estate in Smithy Street in Whitechapel. My room cost £400 a month and despite the flat being grotty, I loved it so much. My room was so tiny that the bedroom door would hit the end of the bed when you opened it and the bed itself was nestled against the wall. This was my first flat in London, which I was paying the rent for from money I earned, and I could smoke in it and have friends round whenever I wanted.

I'd got my pay rise because the startup had just raised its Series A funding. A startup switches gears when it raises its first millions. There are more investors to please and people to hire and the concept of 'growth' takes centre stage. Although it had been hard work and long hours before, something shifted once we got the funding; and as the startup business swelled and the pressure increased, I worked harder and harder. Everything we were doing suddenly felt a lot more serious.

I was addicted to the numbers. When someone on the team said they loved that our job meant we were helping people have enjoyment in their life through their holidays, I remember thinking that was odd. I didn't care about the people booking their holidays. It was just about me and the numbers. Each month, my targets would rise and I'd jump higher to reach them. I never missed my targets. This wasn't a game of making those numbers as high as possible: this was about showing growth. We needed a picture of a smooth growth curve and we needed that picture so we could put it on a PowerPoint slide and ask more venture capitalists for more money. We needed more money to spend on growing that curve even more, so we could go back again, with an even bigger curve and ask for even more money. It didn't matter how much money we were making, it only mattered that the curve was going up; and to this day, that's how startups work. They call it growth, but it's the dogged pursuit of more. Always more.

Once the numbers for the month had been hit, I'd try to delay sales so they'd close in the next month and contribute to the next month's numbers. But the founder was on to me and he wanted as big a number as possible. I wasn't on commission. I wasn't in those meetings with the PowerPoint slides. I didn't get to see how important those numbers were. I simply got high on the rush of seeing my numbers go up and up. Like any addiction, it was fun at first and then I didn't know who I was without it. There were four days to go until the end of the month:

'If you get £5,000 above target this month, I'll…'

'Go on…' I said. I looked up at him and gave him a cocky look, straight in the eye.

'I'll buy you a bear that is bigger than you.'

'Start googling "large bears",' I said.

Three weeks later, the founder dragged a 5ft 5 inch bear into the office.

'I had no idea how expensive these things are,' he said.

The large bear would sit in the corner of our office, moving with us from office to office as we hired more people and needed more space. The bear would slowly waste away over the years, the stuffing would start pouring out of its tummy and legs. It sat slumped against the wall of the office, with its head hanging down to one side. You couldn't see its eyes.

After I moved to Whitechapel, Tony gave me his wife's old bike and so I started cycling to work. On my way to work one day, I abruptly fell over the front of my bike, over the handlebars and into the middle of the street outside the Pret a Manger on Shoreditch High Street. A passer-by pulled me out of the road before the cars behind me ran me over. They left me sat on the chairs outside Pret. I called the American founder to explain why I'd be late, and even though my arm was twisted the wrong way and I couldn't lift it, I got a black cab to the office. My shoulder still twinges from that fall.

The addiction was eroding my body and I was beginning to break. I was gaunt and grey from living off diet coke, cigarettes and the endless packets of crisps in the office. I was also too busy to cook properly in my Whitechapel flat and so would eat either pitta bread and taramasalata or ready-made tortellini pasta. Dean had moved to London after Bristol and told me off for having lost weight.

'We looked after you in Bristol, fed you properly,' he said to me one night.

'I'm fine,' I said.

I got gum disease, and my mouth was sore and bursting with blisters.

'Have you been working too hard or partying too hard?' the dentist asked me.

'You could say that.' I lay there looking up at him and shifted.

I was mortified. I didn't want anyone to know I had this disease. We were at Tony's house on a Sunday for lunch and I had to refuse alcohol because of my antibiotics. I was terrified of them asking why I was on them.

Despite my dedication to those numbers, I was cracking up and my response to the stress was becoming increasingly erratic. I woke up one day and decided I couldn't go into the office and so I told the founders I was ill and stayed at home for two days. It was obvious something was off and people kept asking over Skype chat if I was okay. One of the newer hires at the startup offered to help get me out and I appreciated his offer of help, but the thought of leaving was more terrifying than staying.

I took the payment terminal out with me at weekends and went offline when I should be asleep and then enjoyed the freedom of staying up most of the night with my friends and not having to worry about any emails coming through. Then I'd wake up before my friends, who were usually staying over, to go downstairs and try to clear the bookings email inbox before they got up. We'd then get a Domino's and go for a walk and I'd try juggling my friends, the hangover and bookings for the rest of the day.

The juggle took its toll and after one of those weekends, while standing at the 106 bus stop on Cambridge Heath Road, I snapped at the fourth American founder, who'd joined the company shortly after me and was my bookings manager.

'When, when will this end?' I shouted at him down the phone.

I'd asked to move out of taking bookings and back into the PR and marketing side of the business because I'd had enough and I knew this was breaking me, even though I couldn't stop. The founders agreed and started hiring for my replacement, but I was finding it increasingly hard to manage.

'We're trying our best to hire your replacement,' he told me.

'But when? When am I getting replaced?' I was still shouting. He later told me, kindly, that I could have handled that incident more professionally, but then, once it was all over, he also said he admired my tenacity.

I was finally given a bit of freedom shortly after another bout of reckless behaviour involving the friend of a guy Anna S. had started seeing. My London school friends called him Essex because that was where he was from, and my northern housemates called him Soho Boy because that's where he lived. His friends called him by his surname, Taylor, so I called him that – although I never really used his name in his company as I wasn't sure what to call him and I was always slightly on edge around him.

I was drawn to him, and one night in March 2011 the after party at my flat in Whitechapel turned into a sleepover and I got out of my bed, which I was sharing with Anna C., and went downstairs to lie on the floor next to where he was sleeping. He wrapped his arms around me and I slept on the cold, hard floor of my living room. I was drawn to his other worldliness. He had a young face, but at 28 he seemed a lot older than my 22. He lived on his own in a flat on Berwick Street and he worked at a men's clothing shop on Upper Street. He was very well dressed and he gently made fun of the holes in my clothes, which brought an awareness to my scruffiness which I hadn't noticed before. I was spending my money on rent and going out and I was never near any clothes shops. We all wanted to know how he could afford to live on his own as it seemed so incredibly adult for someone in our orbit to be able to do so. He was such a mystery that he wasn't even on Facebook.

He didn't drink wine with dinner. It was the first time a boy would take me out for dinner and pay, so I'd brush to one side any thoughts I had as he ordered a vodka tonic with his meal. He often drank Smirnoff Ices.

'Why aren't you eating anything?' He asked in the basement of a sushi restaurant on our first date in Soho.

'I can't use chopsticks.'

He laughed. I didn't want to try picking them up again and I didn't want to use my hands or a fork and so I just sat there.

After dinner, I passively followed him around the bars of Soho and we ended up at Trisha's, a hidden bar down some stairs on Greek Street. We went back to his and had the sort of mind-blowing sex that was only possible with a stranger you cared little for. Immediately after it was over, I felt self-conscious and I leapt out of his bed and started putting my clothes back on. I thought it'd be best if I left, even though I wasn't sure how I'd get back to Whitechapel from Soho at 3 a.m. on a weeknight. I knew he had a girlfriend, because Anna S. had told me, and I didn't feel guilty for playing a part in the betrayal against her. I told myself that it wasn't my responsibility, but his. While he didn't mention her all night, I presumed he knew I knew and as I passively followed his lead about where to go in Soho, I also passively followed his lead of not mentioning her in his presence. I found the knowledge of her existence freeing; there was safety to be found in his seeming unavailability. As I rummaged around the end of the bed for my socks, I didn't want him to think I had any expectations from him.

'Where are you going?'

'Home.'

'Don't. Stay.'

He pulled me back into the bed and it felt nice to be wanted.

As I was struggling to use chopsticks and enjoying the warm embrace of a stranger, I was not doing booking sales for the startup. I'd gone off the grid that night and the destructive streak in me that was increasingly rearing its head meant I didn't care at all. The next morning, I brushed my teeth with his toothpaste and my finger, licked my fingers and tried to remove smudge from under my eyes, and took the tube to the office in Farringdon. Eyes flicked up from screens as I walked in and sat down, but nothing was said. I emailed the Annas with the story of the night before and wrote to them:

He's good fun, such a character.

The startup seemed interested in our physical health, so we all did this gruelling thing on a Wednesday evening called Urban Gym, where we'd run around the city, passing the bankers smoking outside pubs and stop at random spaces and do squats and lunges and other awful exercises in the cold. My fitness was not on a par with the men I worked with and so I was jogging and dying at the back of the group when the American founder hung back to jog next to me.

'Hey, so did you have fun last night?' He was barely breaking a sweat and I could hardly breathe.

'Um, yeah.'

'So, you can't just disappear. It makes things difficult for the company.'

'Yeah, that's fair, um, sorry.' I didn't have the words for an excuse.

'Maybe you can give us warning when that's going to happen?'

'I'll try, but I don't always know when it's going to happen.' I hadn't even heard from Taylor yet.

Within a week, I disappeared again for another romp in Soho and I was then told that the American founder's wife was going to cover me on booking sales for one weeknight a week and one weekend day, so I could have the time off. I could just let her know which day and evening I wanted off at the start of the week. So, for a short while, I'd get my one night off a week and I'd spend it with a slightly eccentric guy who drank Smirnoff Ices and had a girlfriend that we never spoke of. Looking back, my state of emotional detachment made me cruel and my lack of empathy for her was chilling. I put loser in front of her name when talking about her to my friends if retelling a story of how I saw something of hers in his flat or if she was calling him when we were together. I liked him enough to keep seeing him and to be disparaging of her, but the knowledge of her existence guaranteed a distance between me and him that I was comfortable with. We don't consciously say to ourselves that we're not letting people get close to us because we're afraid of getting hurt, it's just something that we do.

The affair eventually came to an end in the summer. I never wanted to see him when I had my period, so I'd taken my contraceptive pill back-to-back to avoid getting it, but I'd done it for so long that I suddenly had an ongoing period and, instead of being honest, I dodged and delayed seeing him, hoping it would go away. While avoiding him, I bumped into him when I'd just got back from Secret Garden Party and I was grey and overtired and, ashamed of my appearance, pulled away when he tried to kiss me.

My free evening and weekend day wasn't enough respite, especially as I was using the weekend evening for another sleepless night rather than for rest. But I still couldn't consider leaving the startup. No matter how tired and stressed I was, the pain was something tangible I could make sense of. I was struggling, but it was far more comfortable to place the blame on the enemy of 'work'. Work was the enemy, not me, and I was a victim to it. Shame doesn't allow us to blame others, only ourselves, and the brutality of work, which I saw as something placed on me, was a worthy trade to silence the shame monster that was wrestling inside me, always threatening to bubble to the surface and expose itself.

The new world I'd run off into had not been as fun as I'd hoped and my shame monster was sneaky and always found its way back, no matter how hard I tried to get rid of it. Perhaps it's like taking an addictive drug, where the first few times you take it, it numbs you from your self-hatred and feels amazing and then it stops feeling so good after a while and becomes something that you need to exist and it gnaws at your body and gradually erodes your life. You stop knowing who you are without it and you're afraid to find out. Work was my drug and it was my shield of self-protection because if I was working all the time, I didn't have to relive the torture I'd felt in the summer that shattered another piece of my heart.

Summer 2010

I looked down at my hands. *Oh shit.* I sprinted back up the stairs, ran past the dingy cafe and into the dingier loos and looked at the counter above the sinks. They were gone. How could I have been so careless? How could I have lost the rings? I stood there staring at the counter, as though if I kept staring at it they'd reappear. I'd taken my rings off to wash my hands and forgot to put them back on again, and in the few minutes I'd gone downstairs and ran back up again, they'd gone. I went to ask the ladies at reception if they'd seen them.

'Sorry, darling, nothing's been handed in.'

'I only took them off for a few minutes to wash my hands.'

'You should never take off your rings.'

'I know that now. They weren't expensive, just high sentimental value.'

There was an antiques shop on Cotham Hill in Bristol between our house and the university campus on Woodland Road. I loved it there. I went in and would look at all the precious and old items and play with the rings. On one trip, I couldn't decide between two burgundy rings. They looked great together, but I could barely afford one. I was drawn to them and they made me feel calm. I decided to buy one and then I kept going back to look at the other one, which was more Art Deco in style. I was walking past with Zac one day and asked if I could go and look inside.

'This is the one I love.'

'I might get that for my mum,' he said.

'Oh, that's nice.'

'Her fingers are the same as yours. Try it on so I can see.' He smiled at the shop owner.

'That's so nice you're getting her that. It's such a gorgeous ring.'

When we got home, he handed me the box and a piece of paper fell out.

Love you, silly.

I hadn't dared hope. It hadn't been that long since he'd bought me my Tiffany necklace for Christmas. It was my first (and only) gift I've ever received in one of those famous little blue boxes. He'd been outraged that I'd never owned something from Tiffany & Co. when Tiffany was my name; and since I'd hung the *Breakfast at Tiffany's* poster in my room in first year, he knew I liked things with my name on them. I wore the Tiffany necklace every day. At least when I lost the rings, I still had my silver, twisted Tiffany necklace.

I was so busy and wrapped up in Secret London and the early days of the hospitality startup that I was as careless with Zac as I was with the rings. It wasn't long after our break-up and the dust had settled on the madness of the Secret London weekend that we started talking to each other again. When we were still together, Zac had got us tickets to see The XX at The Shepherd's Bush Empire and I still wanted to go, so we went. As we watched them and I stood in front of him with my lager in a plastic pint cup, he put his arms around me and it was as if nothing had changed.

About a week after seeing The XX, he messaged me on GChat:

Zac: *Can I ask you a question?*

Me: *Yes.*

Zac: *Is there any chance for us ever again?*

Me: *Why are you asking this now?*

Zac: *I think it's pretty obvious that I'm still in love with you.*

I told him that I didn't think anything had changed and so our problems would remain and therefore getting back together would be unlikely.

Zac: *You've changed.*

Me: *Prob in the wrong direction for me and you to work out.*

Zac: *Why are you proud of that?*

Me: *I'm not, I was just saying.*

Zac: *Well if ur not why don't you try and change back?*

That was exactly my fear: that I'd change and go back to who I saw myself as in the eyes of others in third year.

I refused to commit to a time for Zac and me to speak.

Zac: *I'm asking for nothing but you to pick up a phone.*

Me: *Yes okay fine.*
Me: *Night.*

Zac: *Okay I'll ring you Friday night.*

Me: *Not Friday.*
Me: *I told you I'm busy.*

And then he said:

Zac: *Cos at the moment I wander between being sad then being hopeful that we'll get back together*
Zac: *and it's destroying me completely.*

Me: *I'm under lots of stress and don't want to deal with this right now.*

Zac: *You really know how to make me feel like shit on the bottom of your shoe don't you?*

Me: *You really know how to wind me up and upset me at exactly the wrong moments.*

Zac: *Well I've been fucking suicidally depressed for the last 4 weeks so maybe talking may help us both get beyond this.*
Zac: *That's all I'm saying.*

I saw those words as a weapon and not the cry for help that perhaps they were. I glared at them, seeing them as an attack that blamed me for Richard's death and threatened that history was going to repeat itself if I continued to act in this way. A rage washed over me. It was the worst thing he could have said.

Me: *I don't want to talk to you right now because you've been unpleasant and unfair.*

Me: *I'm tired, I need to sleep and you're just piling a load of shit on me.*

I logged off.

This incident was soon forgotten and the tug of war between my new world and my past continued. No matter how hard I tried to abandon my former life, something kept drawing me back to it and I could never fully let go of the thread to it and to my grief that Zac represented, so it wasn't long until I was drawn back to Zac again. By the time of my birthday in June, we were acting like a couple again. I'd talk to him all day on Facebook messenger or GChat and I'd bitch about how tiring and stressful work was. The more I hated the startup, the closer I'd be drawn to him.

Me: *In other news, I need new rings… xx*

Zac: *You are a very needy person. You are lucky you got back with me just before your birthday. Accident? I think not. xx*
Zac: *No fear! Kinda-not-at-all-boyfriend-shaped-person is ON THE CASE! Xx*

The founders had a gift for sensing when I was slipping away and they'd draw me back in with a promise of something new and shiny. In the summer, I had a review and something changed in me. Once again, I cast Zac to one side to focus on work and so the game of ping pong between him and my work continued.

Me: *Sorry I've not been in touch, mad busy at work.*

I'd switched from being available to him to being distant and had absorbed myself back into my work.

> Zac: *I feel I should tell you that I'm not very happy at the moment about us, I'm thinking maybe we should return to being friends if things don't improve.*

> Me: *Are you unhappy with me because I've been a bit out of touch or is it something else? x*

> Zac: *The out of touchness and unwillingness to talk has been difficult, from when you had your review onwards really, and since your birthday it's felt like when we had broken up, it feels like your attention has drifted to other things x*

> Me: *I know I'm busy and distracted. I haven't had a chance to think about it yet but I don't know if I can give you all you need. We can talk later. Hope you enjoy the rest of your day. xx*

> Zac: *Just some thoughts – when you're miserable and bored = getting back together, happy and busy = breaking up. It's the exact same pattern as our relationship. I feel a bit used here – and feel like you've made me look like an idiot. I was happy being single, but came back to you because I felt you needed me, so being ignored and tossed aside the second you feel better is very hurtful. You only seem to be bothered when I'm looking after you, but don't really want to give anything back if it puts you out. This isn't intended to be a mean message, but you should really start thinking about the effects your actions have on other people.*

> Me: *I'm sorry, I can't talk about this now while I'm at work.*

I didn't pay attention to what he was telling me. Looking back now, this was an accurate summary of my selfish behaviour, driven by the constant conflict and struggle I was experiencing between my work and my old life. I liked hiding behind my job. There was virtue to be found in working hard and somehow it excused me behaving badly to those close to me. It seemed reasonable to me to be erratic or distant and to allow my work to consume me. It was convenient for me to believe that work was more important than those I loved. This belief also chimed with the working culture around me where it was expected that work was your priority above all else.

Zac could never forgive me for doing that to him again and I could never forgive him for what would come a few months later. Our Bristol group was going to Bude in Cornwall in July, which was shortly after we'd broken up for the second time. I'd hesitated, but then agreed to go and Zac said he wasn't going to go because he couldn't be around me; then, to my annoyance, he changed his mind last minute and came.

I got to the house in Bude before him and I was sitting on the table outside when he parked up his yellow car and got out of it and walked in. I could see on his face that it hurt him to see me sat there. Within days, we were back sleeping in the same room and acting like a couple again. The group was used to us being together again and spent the rest of the week joking about it. One friend called their Facebook album from the trip 'Zac and Tiffany's dirty weekend away.'

On returning from Bude, we were back talking on GChat all the time and I was staying over at his flat in Willesden Green, which he now shared with Dean and another boy from Bristol. In September 2010, I walked into the Earl of Essex in Islington for our friend Andrew's birthday and I saw Zac standing there with a girl. My heart pounded and I felt hot and shaky as I stood by the door. I wanted to turn around and get out, but it was too late, I'd been seen. Zac and I had slept together days before. I walked in, got a drink at the bar and avoided them for as long as I could.

'Hi.'

'Hi.' He looked to the floor.

'Hi.' I looked her up and down. I noted she was wearing cut-off leggings under a skirt and ballet pumps.

'This is Kate,' Zac said. The horror tore through me and onto my face, which I wished someone would punch.

I left as soon as I could and the darkness inside me vomited up and tore through me. The horror and the pain was soaring as I marched down the streets towards the tube station. Why hadn't I taken the threat that Zac wouldn't always be there seriously? Why hadn't I taken Richard's depression seriously? I'd been careless and the shame monster that'd been gnarling away inside me was right, I wasn't worthy of love and belonging and the rejection of these men proved it. The image of this new girl he'd found to replace me taunted me and I couldn't get her and what she represented out of my head.

Shortly afterwards, we were all going to Bestival festival on the Isle of Wight. I was going with my friends, and Zac was going with his friends and, I found out, he was bringing his new girlfriend. The jealousy consumed me and the obsession swirled around me. It was all I could think about in the run-up to the festival. Every item I packed in my bag and every look or outfit I imagined myself in was for him and her. I was on edge the whole way there, and on the first evening we went to sit at the top of the hill by the main stage. We saw Zac and his friends coming our way and she was with them. The Annas stiffened next to me. Zac walked up the hill and sat next to me, leaving her standing there at the bottom of the hill with his friend, who charmingly led her away from us. Why did it still hurt so much when I just saw how he still loved me and cared so little for her? After a brief and awkward exchange, he got up again and left. Every step I took in that field all weekend I was on high alert that I'd bump into him and her again.

My friends were so patient. I got completely wasted and talked about him, her, her leggings and how could they be here? I was facing the reality that he was no longer there for me and the reality of what I'd done. A part of me died inside and even though it wouldn't be long until we'd be back sleeping together, we'd both inflicted so much irreparable damage on each other. I just couldn't let him go; he hadn't been the one, but he could have been a one. I couldn't lose him like I lost Richard. Shortly after Bestival, Zac uninvited me to his house's party on Facebook, he then GChatted me while I was at work.

Zac: *Hi I feel I should explain? (If you can talk?)*

Me: *This is all I will say*
I have tried to be civil
I cannot help how I felt
It was fucking awful
and I hate you
I hate you for how you made me feel
I hate you for not telling me about it properly
for lying
for making me a fool
for making me feel I had to hide from everything
I fucking hate you
and I cannot believe I went out with you.
That is all.

I didn't hate him at all. What I wanted to say to him was that the pain I felt reminded me of the loss and grief I felt when Richard died. It hurt so much that I couldn't believe I was feeling that again. Heartbreak, shame, grief and rejection are all emotions that hang out at the same family gathering.

We lasted ten days not talking to each other after that GChat exchange. I received an email from him titled:

Dear Tiffany...

There were no words, just links to images. I worried for a moment it was spam, but then I clicked each image link, one by one:

The cover for Blink 182's 'I Miss You'
The poster for the film *In My Life*
A book with the title *Forgive Me My Trespasses*
The cover for Elvis's 'Let's Be Friends'

I sat staring at the images, re-reading them over and over and smiled. As I sat there looking at them, I was taken back to the safety of us together in our rooms on Ashgrove Road in Bristol. Our grief connected us and perhaps, through each other, we were able to stay connected to those who we'd lost that summer of second year at Bristol.

Twenty-seven hours later, I replied:

Ahh, very sweet, it made me smile! Yes, we can be friends. I hope that you are well. X

Zac and his girlfriend broke up shortly after that and by November we were sacking off other events to hang out with each other again. On New Year's Eve, after midnight, Anna S. and I left the party we were at and travelled to his house where there was another party. Midnight had passed and it was already 2011, but we kissed each other a Happy New Year. In January, another work review was looming and I had to fill out a form in advance as things were getting increasingly more professional at the startup. I told him I couldn't think of a weakness to write down. Zac suggested, 'Not following your heart?'

I replied with 'Ha'.

We'd say 'I miss you' when we'd seen each other days before and were seeing each other that night.

Zac: *Why do you want to look good for me anyway?*

Me: *Because obvious.*

Zac: *Why are you getting all silly – you're the only girl for me.*

The review was coming. The pull to be sucked into work was on its way with 2011. The founder gave me a pay rise to £23.5k, said I was now responsible for bookings and told me I could now move out of home. By February I was living in Whitechapel, attached to the payment terminal, addicted to the numbers and not speaking to Zac.

Here's how the narrative is expected to go: I was sad about my dead boyfriend, so I suppressed my feelings by drinking too much (okay, that part is true). So, I partied hard with shallow, vacuous people, who were riddled with their own issues and lack of self-worth. Meanwhile, I abandoned my earnest, puritanical and disapproving friends. I felt better once I stopped. The end.

But for me, in those years, especially during the times that I wanted to escape myself through my work, the partying brought me some of my happiest and calmest moments. I don't look back on that time I spent partying with any regret. Sure, some people came and went and we were young and so we had a disregard for our health and did some stupid, occasionally dangerous things, but the true friends – they were always there, with me. They all came along for the ride and we had a lot of fun together. We had the comfort of one, perfectly sized group, who we knew would gather every weekend and spend the whole time together going on glorious adventures. The club night was no longer the unfamiliar and scary setting it had been in my first experiences of it at Bristol. I grew to love the crowds of people dancing close to each other under the light of the laser beams and I swelled with hope in the toilet queues when I saw girls introducing themselves to each other and sharing eyeliner, like they were destined to be friends for life. I adored the hustle and bustle of the smoking area: it all felt like a second home now.

Once I was tired of dancing, I'd patiently wait, sitting on the floor of the smoking area for my favourite part of the night to come – the after party. There's only been one time in my life when I missed the after party and that was the summer at the end of the first year in Bristol. It was the Bristol Goldney Ball. 'We'll come back, we promise,' Richard and I called back as we ran hand in hand, giggling across the grass, away from the lights of the marquee and the chattering sound of drunk students. We passed out as soon as we got to my bed. I woke up with a bright blue ball gown covering my floor space and a black bow tie resting on top of it. Everyone else had stayed up until sunrise and I enjoyed their stories over breakfast the next day.

But in my twenties, there was no Richard to run off with, and so I never, ever, missed the after party. We'd pile into a cab: the most outgoing friend sat at the front, the smallest in the middle, the other two on either side. The silence increased as the cab drove on and the group's energy waned. We'd arrive at a friend's flat, often mine in Whitechapel, and meet the others who'd follow on in cabs. We'd break out the drinks, dump the ash tray in the middle of the table and the fun would begin again. We'd talk. We'd really talk. About love, life and what it all means. It would be the only time I'd become even close to whispering his name. One morning I was sat on a balcony with Anna C. and I looked ahead over the streets of East London, took a drag of my cigarette and said:

'I really miss him.'

'I know.'

We'd also get quite cold in my dingy flat and I'd run up and down the stairs to get jumpers for my friends; and before we knew it. we'd be wrapped in multiple layers on the sofa. We'd gossip about the night while we were still technically in it.

'How we doing for cigarettes?'

'It's fine, I've got loads.'

'Are you sure?'

'Yeh, what's mine is yours. More whiskey?'

'Go on then. Gosh, imagine a world where smoking didn't kill you.'

'Yeah, but maybe that world would have no whiskey in it too.'

One by one, people would peel off, as the sun would shine brighter in the sky. But the after party never truly ended. I'd always end the night with at least one friend in my bed. We'd wake up the next day, eat a Domino's and then wander around East London. Depending on the weather, we'd drink cider in the park, or pints in the pub. My old friends were always there, but I also made new friends during that time, some I'm still so close to today. So even though partying hard while working hard wasn't the best thing for my health, I see those friends and the time I spent with them as a saviour. Without those moments, all I'd recall would be an addicted blur, tied to my phone, the computer screen and those numbers.

In September 2011, the startup found someone to replace me and I was taken off bookings and moved back to marketing and

PR, which meant that I got my evenings and weekends back. The company kept growing and had become a bit of a darling of the startup scene. It was still the early days of 'Silicon Roundabout', the name given to London's answer to Silicon Valley, as most startups were gathered around the Old Street roundabout.

'Silicon Roundabout' was still in its humble beginnings, as there weren't that many London startups yet, so any job they'd advertise would get inundated with applicants who wanted to break free from corporate life because startups looked fun from the outside. The company's expansion was fast. It felt sudden, almost as if it had happened overnight. It had been me and the founders for almost a year and then, within weeks, we had 20 people in March and by September it was somewhere between 30 and 40 people. The interview process to get in was rigorous and everyone who joined had overcome many hurdles to get there.

I was enjoying this constant stream of new people and it meant that there was a whole new social scene opening its doors to me. Startups encourage you to socialise with each other and so while my job was operating at more normal office hours, I was giving my spare time over to the startup in a different way. Friday night drinks became the most fun events in the world and I began to abandon my friends to spend more and more time with my colleagues.

I enjoyed my reinvention and feeling like a different person so much that I wanted to look different too, so I dyed my dark brown hair blonde in December 2011. I looked different, I felt different and what Zac had said was right, I had changed. But the shedding of myself only managed to last for so long. The past always finds a way of catching up with you and the shame monster is always waiting to pounce.

Chapter 10

The Table

'Should we just get the cab to go back to yours?'

'Sure.'

'Because it'll cost a fortune to go to Stepney then Seven Sisters.'

My hand was clutching the yellow handlebars and my head was leaning against the window of the cab. I looked up at him.

'Yes, you can stay over.' I smiled.

'We'll put pillows down the middle of the bed so we don't touch each other,' he said.

'Reckon I can't resist you? Hahaha. Bit weird, but sure.'

I was drunk, but I could tell he was embarrassed. He was always a bit awkward and I enjoyed winding him up.

'I certainly can't resist you in that damn duffel coat,' I said and started laughing. He went redder and reiterated that he was putting pillows down the middle of the bed.

'Seriously, whatever. Do what you want with the pillows. What a night. I couldn't see straight at one point.'

There was a level of drunk I got with my colleagues that I didn't get to with my old friends; perhaps this was why I was increasingly prioritising getting wasted with workmates above seeing my friends. Work drinks offered pure, reckless escapism where there was a thrill to be found in crossing boundaries and where I abandoned consideration of the consequences of my actions. I didn't even think about what it might mean that I was in this black cab with a colleague who was coming back to mine. After we jumped in the cab together, we waved to the rest of our colleagues, who were standing outside The Star of Kings on York Way, giving little thought to what they'd think of us leaving together. We'd been dancing for hours in The Star's basement club. I was on the whiskey that night and I'd been bumping and grinding with an assortment of male colleagues on the dancefloor. The club floor was sticky and the whole night had a foreboding messiness to it. This 'living in the moment' attitude I'd adopted on the surface appeared like the behaviour of someone who was free, when, in reality, I was trapped. Shame snarled around my belly, my soul was adrift and I discovered a temporary ointment in the sharp draw of the whiskey and the thrill in acting as if I didn't care about anything at all. I put on such a good act that I had myself fooled.

We got out of the cab on my street, which was on the Stepney Green end of Globe Road. Our Whitechapel landlord had wanted to increase our rent, so we'd moved to a much nicer and bigger house that month. I dropped my keys on the floor as I tried to put them in the door.

'Shhh,' I said and laughed as we climbed the stairs, passed the never-ending hanging laundry and walked into my room. I went to the loo, got back and he'd laid the pillows in the middle of the bed.

'Ha, okay.'

I got into the bed with all my clothes on and lay there for a millisecond before we turned towards each other and leaned in to kiss each other at the same time. We threw the pillows off the bed.

The next morning, I woke up with a sore throat and a sticky mouth. He was already out of the bed.

'Which one in the bathroom is your toothbrush?' he asked. I was startled by the familiarity that came from that question.

'Um. It's the electric Philips one.'

He went to brush his teeth, came back and stood awkwardly by the bed and waved at me.

'Bye Francis,' I croaked back.

I heard the front door close and let out a big sigh, put a pillow under my head and lay there staring at the ceiling. Everyone said this was going to happen. The office had been making jokes about us since he'd joined the company. I was too hungover to think about it properly but then couldn't stop thinking about what had happened. It was Saturday and I spent the rest of the day lying in bed and drinking orange squash so I could recover in time to go out again. That night, I went to a house party with Anna S. and some of her friends. I told them what had happened the previous night.

'It's really weird, I always just thought he was a bit of a geek who I'd just hang out with when no one else was around, but I feel like I really like him,' I said to Anna S. and her housemate while we were sat on someone's living room floor. I found some excitement in the drama of sleeping with a colleague. It gave me something to think and talk about that distracted me from a life where I was feeling deeply unfulfilled. I found many thrills in drama over these years as it helped play into my avoidance of the reality of the depth of the sadness of my emotions.

'Won't it be awkward on Monday?' Anna S. said.

'Probably, hahaha.'

'Pass us the light that's over there, will you?'

I was excited to go to work on Monday. The anticipation trickled through my body as I sat at my desk and waited for him to come in. I was in far earlier than usual. Francis was in a different department from me, so he sat a few rows away, but my desk was positioned so I could see him in my eye line. Shortly after 9.30, I saw him come through the office door and I felt a sudden rush. I tried desperately not to look up or move my eyes off my screen as he walked over to his desk. The main garage office had been turned into a place where the operations team sat and they'd made some of the space into a warehouse, so us office workers were crammed together in a very small office on the second floor of the main building. I got up from my desk to get some water from the water cooler, still feeling self-conscious of every movement I made, and I tried to keep my eyes fixated on my glass as it filled with water. My heart was pounding as I sat back at my desk.

Then he started acting like a prick and I would sit at my desk emailing my friends about how upset I was. He kept sending me annoying messages over Skype instant messenger chat, which is what we all used to communicate in the office. He'd send links to clothes and shoes and ask if I thought he should buy them. It seemed as if he was going out of his way to make his disinterest clear and it stung. He talked to me about dates he was going on and girls he was seeing and the more he did so, the more I was drawn to him. He offered to show me a picture of a girl he was going on a date with who he'd met on OkCupid and I had to say yes, I wanted to see her photo, to show him that I didn't care.

Anna S. replied to my email when I told her about this saying:

> *Do you know what they call dickheads in America? Juiceboxes.*
> *I really like that. Francis is being a total juicebox.*

Francis continued to be a juicebox and I continued to care. In March, in my house in Stepney Green, we had a house party and it was one of the best parties we'd ever thrown. We had three DJ sets and the whole ground floor was bursting with people dancing to the music. People were spilling over our staircases and our garden was packed with smokers, with their bodies draped around our brown leather sofas, which we'd moved outside. A group of colleagues from the startup had come and they were dancing away together in a circle. Anna S.'s favourite song, Azealia Banks' '212' came on and I ran over to dance with her as she mouthed away the song lyrics. I paused as I spotted Francis through the throng of people talking to a girl who was wearing what looked like a dead fox around her neck. I watched him follow her out and leave through the front door. I ran upstairs, opened the door to my bedroom, which was filled with some of my closest friends, who often preferred to retreat and chat at a party rather than be in the main part of it, and I slumped onto the middle of the bed and bitched about how I'd been rejected for a girl who was wearing a dead fox around her neck. I missed Anna C. so much at that moment. She'd moved to New York to study at Columbia Journalism School and I wanted my party buddy, who was so often always by my side. As my room cleared out and, one by one, people went home, Zac was one of the few people left over. I went to sit close to him on the floor, with our backs leaning against the wall. I hadn't seen him much in the past year, but we'd remained loosely friends through the group and he always came to my parties.

'Will you stay? I don't want to be alone when everyone's left,' I asked him.

'Yes, of course.'

'Not in a sex way, though.'

'Okay.'

The sun was up and everyone had gone. We got into my bed, he spooned me and I fell asleep.

I felt lonely one Wednesday evening, so I set up a *Guardian* Soulmates profile. I didn't want to do it. I thought online dating was weird and Francis was the only person I knew who did it, and people in the office laughed at him about it. Surely, I should just be able to meet people in real life like everyone else? But I hadn't met anyone and I'd had another annoying interaction with Francis that day and I didn't want to feel alone anymore. We'd gone to Leather Lane to get lunch together and he told me how he was going on another date that night and that he'd got back with the girl that he was seeing around the time he and I had thrown the pillows off the bed and first slept together. He told me how he felt bad about 'the other people he'd shagged', which included me. My cheeks burned as he said those words as we were walking and his arms were crossed around his chest as he said it. We sat down in a park outside to eat our lunch. I was still burning from when he said that he regretted shagging me. It further perpetuated the worthlessness I felt at his ambivalence towards me. I lashed out.

'So, I got this super weird message from Andreas last night.' Andreas was on Francis's team.

'Really?' His mouth was wrapped around his fat burrito and he was chewing down on it, fast and the juice was spilling out of the sides of his mouth. I could tell I didn't have his full attention, but I continued.

'Yeh, he like messaged me really late at night on Facebook after that night out the other day, being all like "I have a few things I want to talk to you about." What do you think he'd want to talk to me about? Weird, right?' I had a strong idea. I'd been drunkenly flirting with him that night and he'd asked me if Francis and I had had sex and I'd said yes.

'What do you think it could be?'

Not much of Francis's burrito was left. He wiped his mouth with a napkin and said, 'You're working your way through my team.' He laughed and went back to his burrito.

I stared back at him. I was stunned, my story had backfired and I was hurt by his words again. Then he said, 'It should really be awkward between us.'

This was followed by an awkward silence.

'Well, I guess there's nothing to say really,' I replied, trying to sound casual and light-hearted. He'd been making it clear he wasn't interested and I was determined he wouldn't pick up on an inkling of the truth that I'd been emailing my friends about every single thing he'd said to me the last few weeks.

'I'm not good at talking about stuff,' he joked.

'Yeah me neither… but unlike with others I'd drunkenly slept with, I didn't want to avoid you or never see you again, though…' I thought he'd given me a window of opportunity and I was taking it by testing the waters. I still had some hope. But then, he simply said, 'Hmm, yeah,' and started to stand up as he'd finished his burrito, when I hadn't finished mine.

'Should we head back?'

We started walking back and I threw the rest of my burrito in the bin. I'd have saved myself a lot of time if I'd spoken to Francis directly about liking him. Even now, I hate to admit that was the case.

Shortly after this conversation, I went to San Francisco with my friend Jack from school days for my first real holiday in two years. I'd hired an intern to help me with PR, turned the emails off on my phone and left her to it as Jack and I spent two weeks travelling around California. The trip had been Jack's idea as it wouldn't have crossed my mind to do anything like that, and I was so thankful he'd brought me along. It was a joyful holiday as I detached myself from my work and followed Jack's lead to go with the flow. We planned what we did and where we stayed as we went, and although things would often go wrong, they would always work themselves out and I learned that there was fun to be had with friends and in relinquishing control. On the flight to Las Vegas, which we'd almost missed, I asked Jack what I should do about Francis.

'You either talk to him about your feelings or get over it.'

'I'm not going to talk to him. Give me another option.'

'There isn't another option.'

'For fucks sake, I can't do it. I can't talk to him about it.'

'That's it then.'

I wanted to keep analysing Francis's every move and Skype message on the plane journey, but knew I'd already pushed the boundaries for how much time I could obsess for and I didn't want Jack to regret coming away with me on this trip, so I left it. Talking to Francis was too terrifying, so I'd made my choice and I was going through my pictures on Facebook to pick some for my *Guardian* Soulmates profile. Such was my lack of enthusiasm for joining *Guardian* Soulmates, I never went back on it again and the night before my twenty-fourth birthday, on a Friday after work drinks, Francis was back in my bed.

The next night was my birthday party and we had friends round at our house. I was standing next to Zac in the kitchen.

'You got a boyfriend yet?' He always asked me this question in that way.

'I've met someone actually.'

He swallowed. 'Who?'

'Well, you already know them, they left earlier.'

Francis had come to the party and left early, which confused me at first, but then I thought it was good in a way. I walked him to the door and said goodbye. We hesitated and went for a hug. This time felt different.

Zac straightened himself up as he'd been leaning on the kitchen counter. 'Is it Jack?'

'No, no, it's Francis from work.'

'Is he as obsessed with that startup as you?'

'Pretty much. It's all he talks about really.'

'Great. You've made it your whole world now.'

'Shut up.'

Zac stayed over that night.

He was right, Francis and I talked about work all the time and not much else. Our bond was formed through an exploration of work gossip rather than an exploration of each other. I often wondered throughout our relationship if he was just with me so he could talk about the startup to someone who knew the characters in his stories. I'm not sure what was different about the drunken hook-up that happened that Friday before my birthday party, but we kept doing it, and by August I was lying on the grass at Wilderness Festival because I needed to rest for a bit. I felt sick and I thought I heard him say he loved me, but I was too scared to check if that's what he said. Shortly after that, he became increasingly stressed about people finding out about us at work. His concern was bugging me. He also seemed disproportionately perturbed by me smoking. There was a cruel night where he'd come to the Genesis cinema in Whitechapel with me and my flatmates and after the film, one of my housemates offered me a cigarette and I accepted. When we got home, he was mad.

'That cigarette was unnecessary,' he said.

'I know. I've cut down so much. Is that not enough?'

He said he wasn't going to kiss or touch me so I'd learn my lesson. We lay there in bed, side by side, him rejecting my advances, as I kept trying to reach over to him. His body remained stiff. The craving for warmth and loneliness I felt kept me up all night. The withdrawal of the physical touch felt like a physical pain and I thought that that was perhaps all I deserved, and not just because I'd smoked that cigarette. The feelings of abandonment as he lay there, stiff, fed my shame monster and as it gnarled away at me I grew increasingly panicked. I lay awake thinking of every mistake and rejection I'd had in my life. I thought of Richard and wished he were alive, but the feeling of the emotional and physical recoil of Francis bubbled up so much self-hatred that I thought I understood why Richard had left me. It was a horrible night and I feel sick revisiting it.

I wish I'd held on to how awful I'd felt that night. I wish I'd held on to how cold someone could be when I needed warmth more than anything because I was already cold enough to myself. Perhaps me being drawn to him for his coldness was a way to be cruel to myself. Prior to him, I was in a clichéd pattern of making myself available only to the unavailable men – although the language of someone being either 'available' or 'unavailable' was something I'd only learn years later in therapy. What it meant in the language of a 23-year-old was that I'd often end up sleeping with men who had girlfriends and then lusting after them after their seamless disposal of me. One of these men once said I reminded him of the character played by Sarah Michelle Gellar in *Cruel Intentions*. In contrast with the blonde and innocent character played by Reece Witherspoon, Gellar's character is twisted and manipulative and her downfall could be considered a cautionary tale for brown-haired girls who are too overt in their sexiness. She ends the film, crying, humiliated and alone. I accepted that it was plausible that this was my destiny.

I suspect that there were some good, 'available' people who slipped by over those years. I don't know if it was persistence or us being flung together in the confines of the office, but somehow the one who was disinterested in me and was the subject of so many frustrated emails to my friends became my boyfriend, albeit a secret one at first.

The whole office eventually found out about us because we had a blazing row on Old Street during a party at Look Mum No Hands! to celebrate the startup's third birthday in September 2012. A girl from the operations team who I'd barely spoken to, but who was known as a trouble maker, told him I'd said bad things about him to her. He believed her and not me, and for some unknown reason he chose to bring this up with me at the company party when we were both very drunk.

'I don't even fucking speak to her,' I shouted at him outside on the street, not too far from some smoking colleagues.

'Well, that's the point.'

'How is that the fucking point? If you think I'm some kind of bitch, that's a different issue.'

And then because we were both so wasted, the argument escalated into nonsensical ranting and I ended up shouting at him about how much I'd invested in this relationship and how done I was.

'I'm done. I'm done,' I screamed. The colleagues loitering nearby were looking down at their cigarettes. I ran off and Francis eventually followed me. I later found out that our friends had told him to go after me when he'd gone back into the party. When I later found that out, I was humiliated that he hadn't come after me of his own accord. He caught up with me as I'd hailed a black cab and was standing there, with the cab door wide open, waiting to escape into it. I burst into tears and eventually slammed the door closed and walked off with him instead of getting in the cab.

It was a sheepish return to my desk on Monday morning. My manager, who was the latest head of marketing (we got through a few during my time), said to me as soon as I sat at my desk, 'So, we can stop pretending we don't know about you and Francis now, then?'

The dumping from Francis was sudden. He called me and said that we were too different, that he didn't think it was going to work longer term and that's why he'd been hesitant for people at work to find out about us. Ultimately, he said, it came down to how he liked skiing and I didn't.

After Francis dumped me for not being a skier, I cried all day, followed my housemate Evi around the Co-op in Stepney Green and bought a packet of Marlboro Lights as a fuck you to him. I came back home and went to bed and lay there for the rest of the day, too teary to do anything. In the evening, Evi knocked on my door and her head peered round.

'There's someone here to see you,' she said.

I saw Francis's sheepish face as she opened the door wider. My first thought was that I was worried that I looked awful. He walked into the room and sat on my chair in the corner and I stayed propped up on the bed. He started crying and saying he'd made a mistake. His cheeks were even redder than usual. He said he was on the phone to his parents and they'd given him a talking to, saying he'd seemed happy with me and that he was turning 30 soon and many of his friends were already married, so perhaps it was time to settle down. I was too young to be able to relate to this as lots of my friends were still single and I didn't know anyone who was even considering marriage. I said I wasn't sure about getting back together and how would I know this wouldn't happen again? I felt beaten and shaky for days after, but I slowly let him back in. I kept saying to my friends that I didn't trust he could fix it. He thought that everything was now fine. We never really spoke of it ever again and we eventually settled back into a new routine of togetherness, but I never truly let that incident go.

We got to that point you get to in a relationship when it becomes inconvenient that you don't live together. Even if you leave a toothbrush at their house, it's still a hassle trying to plan your next 48 hours and pack a pair of knickers, and you always forget something important like your mascara. One night, Francis suggested that we move in together and he said that he'd already started looking at flats that we could move into. I hated going to the warehouse where he lived in Seven Sisters. The parties in the building on a Saturday night were so loud that we couldn't sleep at all, the bathroom was gross and had so many toiletries in it, you'd think one hundred people lived there, and the walk from the station to his flat was scary. He also had a flatmate who openly hated me because Francis had had a thing with her friend that had ended around the time I came along and she made no effort to hide her dislike of me. If moving in with him meant I didn't have to go there anymore, I was in.

Somewhere between the day I was dumped and when he said he wanted us to live together, he engaged with our relationship with a new enthusiasm. We shared a passion for tech and little else, and he sent me an invite to the new Find My Friends app, which meant we could see each other's locations at all times, even though we were always in the same place as each other anyway. We shared our Google Calendars, so we could see each other's plans and make plans for each other. We wrapped our lives around each other as we became increasingly intertwined. He started, to my disgust, calling me 'baby'. I let out a protest to this nickname and he said, 'That's what I call my girlfriends.'

My skin crawled every time he said it.

'Because you're my baby.'

It wasn't even an original nickname for me. He'd literally said that to his ex.

As his enthusiasm for the relationship grew, mine waned, but it was fun to have a boyfriend. I liked weekends away at The Pig in the New Forest. It felt grown up, at 25, to be choosing a flat, rather than moving into a flat share that chose me because the price was right and I knew people who needed a housemate. I liked having someone to go home with at night rather than returning to an empty bed. It was nice to have someone to watch TV with, even though sometimes it was annoying that he wouldn't want to watch what I wanted. It was nice to have someone to run across the street to get you a whole fruit and nut Dairy Milk or Mint Aero when you were feeling sorry for yourself. All the lifestyle aspects of our relationship were nice enough, but there was still something wrestling inside me.

Francis lacked life experience and I never could let it go. His lack of life experience was something I came back to over and over again and it would particularly rear its ugly head when I was angry at him, which was increasingly often as time went by. A resentful rage would bubble up inside me. I hated that he wasn't carrying around the heavy darkness that was inside me. He often joked that he started going out with me when I was blonde and I therefore had to stay blonde to keep the relationship. I interpreted this as him not wanting to see the real, brown-haired, darker me.

I often referred to how he saw life through a simple lens of everything being either black or white. But then there was also something about his apparent innocence that attracted me to him, too. It allowed us to exist in a relationship on a surface level, so as we weaved through the societal view of a healthy relationship through achieving milestones, I could keep the monster bubbling up inside me hidden. And yet, although I was an active participant in the concealment of myself, I was pissed off that he'd never felt the pain I had. I was pissed off that he didn't want to see my pain, my darkness, or my brown hair, either.

There is one date a year that I can't ignore and that is Richard's birthday, which was on the 25th February. In the build-up to the date, I think increasingly of him and get agitated from the thoughts. I think of his parents. I remember how his birthday was always a big celebration in our group because another one of our housemates shared the same birthday. I can't help but imagine what could have been if he'd been alive to turn the age he was supposed to be that day.

At that point in my life, he would have been 25. When I was a 19-year-old student, I thought 25 was a very adult age. I told people I expected we'd be married by the time we were 25. On his birthday, I think what our life together would have been like and I fantasise about boring things like doing our laundry. I wonder if I'd have been restless from being with the same person from such a young age. Maybe I wouldn't have appreciated what we had. How could I have, without the knowledge of what it's like when it's taken away?

I mentioned to Francis in passing that evening that this was a difficult day for me. This was the first time I'd mentioned Richard to him, but I didn't tell him Richard's name or how he'd died. 'My boyfriend who'd died at university' was all I said. Francis stood there and went red, he shifted uncomfortably and I turned and retreated away from him like a wounded animal. I couldn't stand to see that expression again. It was the same expression I saw time and time again after Richard died. I could see on Francis's face that he, like many others, found my grief uncomfortable. I dared not add the layer of suicide which, I knew from experience, would have made his face turn to even more discomfort and panic, such is the stigma of death by suicide. Seeing the fear in his eyes made me feel so, so alone.

I changed the subject and never mentioned that I struggled with the 25th February to anyone again. Richard's Facebook page was still up and so I knew many people in my life who were still his Facebook friends would get the notification on his birthday. Although no one ever said anything to me about it, I craved for people to see on Facebook that it was his birthday and pause and think of him. However, I presumed that they didn't and that Richard had been so easily forgotten.

Francis and I moved into a flat between Stoke Newington and Clapton on Evering Road. The tables had always been turning between us since he'd dumped me for being bad at skiing and his parents had told him not to, but the tables fully turned shortly after we moved into Evering Road. On the day we moved, I posted a picture of our new flat on Instagram. In the picture, the living room was completely empty apart from one picture on the fireplace, where I'd placed a picture Daneal had given me for my twenty-fourth birthday, while we were housemates in Stepney Green. It was a black and white picture of Richard and me and some of our university friends sat outside in a park drinking on a summer's day. When Daneal had given it to me, it was a beautiful moment of acknowledgment and I cherished the picture for years. It's the only item that's travelled with me through all my frequent house moves. It's the picture that sits in my room today. I placed Richard front and centre, on the mantelpiece in our living room on Evering Road and nothing was ever said about it.

Shortly after moving into our flat, Francis and I had some friends round. During the evening, they went outside for a cigarette. Francis and I came out with them. I took a cigarette off my friend. I lit it, looked Francis in the eye and said, 'What are you going to do about it?'

He didn't reply.

I continued to smoke socially around him, daring him to say anything or do what he'd done before, but he never did. I continued to lash out. I began to find him annoying. I sometimes would still be invited to London openings because of Secret London and I found him embarrassing and uncool if I took him to one. He talked about work all the time. I was finding work unbearable and I didn't want to hear about it when I got home. We'd cycle to work together, have our sad, ham and cheese sandwich of a packed lunch together, cycle home together and then I'd listen to him talk about work in the evenings. I couldn't stand it. The intensity of this monotony was waking up my shame monster.

Work became a place of torment rather than refuge. As the company grew, it felt as if I was in a constant game of chess. The firings were frequent and while people coming and going is a natural part of startup life, seeing others lose their jobs put everyone on edge. Every day felt like a race. 'Move fast and break things' was the famous Facebook motto that captured the mood of this era of startup land perfectly. Except, in our case, we were trying to move fast, but without breaking things, because we were afraid of the consequences of failure.

I began to think I was going crazy. I considered that I must be the problem or that I was making it up in my mind and I was seeing things that weren't there. Whether true or not, my fears became a self-fulfilling prophecy as I was crumbling under the pressure and my reputation was going with it. I became hypersensitive to any negativity at the startup. Work was meant to be my safe place, where I'd gone to hide from my problems, but it had become the problem. I lost my confidence and was convinced everyone hated me and that I'd be fired soon. The startup had launched in New York a year or so prior. I always loved flying off to the change of scene and the smaller, friendlier office, and my next trip to New York, the one which would change everything, was approaching.

Until that trip to New York, 'I'd never cheat' is the sort of thing I used to say about myself. I'm always suspicious of people who say they'd never cheat because I'm mistrusting of how they can confidently predict their actions in this way and I notice that as I get older and people develop more experience of life, I hear it said less and less often. When people say they'd never cheat, what I think they often mean is that if they were in the situation, with someone who wasn't their partner and the opportunity to cheat was presenting itself to them, they'd say no. Or perhaps they believe that they wouldn't let themselves get into that situation in the first place. Either way, they're telling us that their moral standards are high and if ever tested, they'd pass. People who say they'd never cheat are wrong because the cheating doesn't happen in the moment when you're with the person you could do the cheating with. Cheating is never a rational decision made in the moment. The act of cheating comes a lot later than the unconscious decision to cheat. The decision to cheat happens before you've even met the person you're going to cheat on your partner with. It happens when you're experiencing the warning signs that the relationship is dying and you're feeling lonely, lost and frightened of the unknown alternative life without this relationship. Cheating starts when you're back at home with the partner who no longer spoons you as you fall asleep and wakes up early to go for a run before you're awake. Cheating can happen when you notice they only go down on you once a month at best, and only once you've had a shower and they expect you to be grateful for it, even though they shove their penis in your mouth every time you have sex, although sex, too is increasingly rare and mechanical. Cheating happens when you notice your partner makes a lot of noise when they eat and you struggle to concentrate when they're talking to you. It happens when you feel misunderstood by them, but you don't want to give them the chance to know you either, because you've lost all hope for their ability to understand you anyway.

Cheating happens when you're unhappy in your relationship and unhappy in yourself. Since I was a teenager, I'd developed a taste for the freedom from my overwrought brain that alcohol provided. As I was increasingly struggling with work, I was looking for other avenues to chase the high of escapism I so consistently craved, and the freely poured spirits at the dive bars in New York were happy to assist me on this mission. The spirits channelled the escapism down my neck and I ran carelessly around the streets of New York. I was running from a latent anxiety that was crawling around me. I was fearful of my shame monster and I was fearful of opening the Pandora's box of my feelings. I wouldn't let anything else run through my head beyond a desire to escape. I found myself caring little for the situation I was in. New York bars never close, so there is no excuse to go back to anyone's apartment, and yet that's what I did on two consecutive nights, with two different men. With each one, I went back to theirs, said no to sex, but kissed them while passing out drunk in their beds. On one of those nights, I woke up in the middle of the night and ran to my phone which was in the middle of the floor and turned off the Find My Friends app in case Francis opened the app and saw that I was far from where I was supposed to be staying.

I flew back on a red-eye flight and walked into our flat on Evering Road early on a Thursday morning. I breathed a sigh of relief as I unlocked the door when I saw that his bike was gone as that meant he'd already left for work. I walked through the door, down the corridor and past the living room. I did a double-take.

He'd finished it. I walked into the living room and stared at it. It was in the middle of the room. It was grand and it was beautiful. It was exactly as I wanted it to be. It could seat 12 people. It looked real and earthy. The longer I stared at it, the more earnest and innocent it seemed. I suddenly felt that the table was judging me. There was a note written on a spare piece of wood lying on top of it:

I hope you love this table as much as I love living with you.

I stood there for a moment and panicked as the guilt kicked in. My phone was in my right hand. I took a step back, lifted my hand and pointed the phone at it. I took a photo and I uploaded it to Instagram.

And I arrive home to a surprise table, made just for me (and guests)

Within minutes, 14 likes. Comments:

That boy. What a talent.

Everyone was talking about the table. They still do:
'Are you going to have a chapter called "The Table" in your book?'
'Fuck off, Zac.'

I was an enthusiastic Instagram user for the couple of months that followed that post: a selfie of us on Halloween, a selfie of us having a dinner party surrounded by all our friends on the table built just for me, we're at the pub for drinks, we're at a wine bar for drinks, we're having drinks on the table, here's some flowers on the table, *our first* Christmas tree #fuckyes.

I was surprised how guilty I felt after that trip to New York for what I'd done. It's all I could think about whenever I looked at Francis and it was eating me up inside. The guilt was providing oxygen to my monster and the self-loathing was bubbling up inside me as if my insides were turning rotten. I bought him an expensive coat which was too cool for him for his birthday and that didn't make me feel better either. I found vindication in the bath mats.

It was just before we were both going to our homes for Christmas and we were sitting side by side on the sofa and I was about to open the first of my Christmas presents. I calmly tore at the wrapping paper and white towels started to peek through. They fell out of the paper, out of my lap and onto the floor. I stared down at the bath mats.

'Do you like them?'

I picked them up off the floor and rubbed their thin material between my fingers.

'See, it's fun! I got you a present for each room in the flat.'

Years ago, Zac played a prank on me when it was our first Christmas together as a couple. He gave me a series of shitty presents, which were good enough to be convincing, but bad enough that I felt silly for politely feigning pleasure on receiving them. He then revealed my true, hugely generous gifts of a pair of Jack Wills tracksuit bottoms and silver Paul Smith stud earrings. I wondered if Francis was maybe playing this trick on me, too.

I unwrapped the next gift. I turned the frame in my hands. It was from IKEA.

'Oh, look, a photo of me and my girlfriends at Wilderness and you're right there in it. Just sitting in the middle of us.'

'Yes, that one is for the bedroom, and then now this present…' He plopped it into my lap. This one wasn't wrapped. '…is for the kitchen…' It was a Leon cookbook. 'My brother has it and I've loved what he has cooked me from it and so I've wanted it for ages.'

'Cool. That's great. Thanks. I'm going to go put this framed picture in the bedroom now.'

I got up and walked into our bedroom. I stood there, staring down at the floor. The bath mats represented everything that was wrong. My mind whizzed: he is bland and cheap and he lacks imagination. He doesn't see me for who I really am. He doesn't understand me. He's a weak person for not wanting to look deep into my soul. It is his fault. It's his fault for not wanting to accept my past and my ugly self. He doesn't love me. If he loved me, he wouldn't buy me bath mats for Christmas. If he loved me, he'd want to see me whole and dark and with brown fucking hair. If he loved me, he'd put the toilet seat down. I began shaking.

'You okay in there?'

'Yes. Coming!'

Shortly after Christmas, he went skiing with his friends. I didn't want to go and when he got back it's all he could talk about.

'Yeah, it was alright, but everyone else had their girlfriends or wives there. Jenny had a great time, even though she's not been skiing before. She had lessons every day.'

I said nothing.

'I was the only one who didn't have their girlfriend or wife there and it was embarrassing. Everyone kept asking why you weren't there.'

'Right, okay.' I turned around and walked off into the bedroom, leaving him alone in the hallway to take his ski jacket off.

I surrendered shortly after the new year. At the sound of my alarm every morning, my body would feel heavy and it hurt to open my eyes. Slowly, painfully, I'd lift my arm to hit the snooze button. I'd do this every eight minutes for over an hour, until I finally turned to my side and pushed my upper body with both of my hands to sit up. One foot at a time, I'd place my feet on the floor. I'd stand up, with my eyes still like slits, not wanting to let the day in. I'd barely get ready: I'd slowly take clothes off the floor and put them on. I'd walk out of the bedroom, while tying my hair up, and Francis would be waiting for me in the hallway. He'd gone for a run, had his breakfast and coffee and looked young and alive. As we'd push our bikes out of the door, I'd pass the mirror. I looked old. I looked tired. I was done. I'd cycle slowly and far behind him: the turn of each pedal was a ginormous effort. As I made each turn, I wondered if I might get run over.

I'd get to my desk and stare at my screen. I didn't want to speak to anyone and I'd keep my headphones in all day. I would go through the motions of the day – reply to some emails, sit in meetings, update a spreadsheet – until it was time to go home again. I could sense people were scared of me and didn't know how to talk to me and I didn't know what to do about their fears because I could barely understand what was happening myself. All I knew was that I wanted to be left alone.

It was 23 January 2014, when the crying couldn't stop. As we were both about to take the right turn to stop outside our office on St John Street, I stopped in the middle of the road.

'I'm sorry, I just can't go in there,' I said, and I didn't hear his reply as I pelted down the road, cycling the fastest I had in my life with no idea where I was heading.

Rain started to pour down on me, heavy rain, that we don't get so often in London – rain where the showers get you instantly, soaking you. Drenched through, I stopped and locked my bike outside a café on a quiet side street in Shoreditch and I went inside, got a coffee and sat at the window staring at my bike. I took a photo of the bike and uploaded it to Instagram:

My bike and me in Shoreditch.

No one from work asked where I was and I didn't tell anyone where I'd gone. I sat there at the café window for hours, refreshing my Instagram page to see if my bike photo was getting any likes.

Chapter 11

Black Coffee

June 2014 (six months later)

'This is for you.'

One of the Harvard graduates handed me a massive cardboard box.

'Cool, thanks.'

I swivelled my chair around, took the box off her and put it down on the floor. Chloe and Brian turned around in unison and then the three of us leant over the box, staring down at it.

'Oooh, someone's got a really big birthday present,' Chloe said with a wide grin. Her pearly-white teeth shone out of her mouth.

'Yeh, weird. I can't think who it'd be from,' I replied, in a tone that didn't match the enthusiasm of hers. I had an inkling who it was from, which is why I was delaying opening it. The box sat there and waited in front of my feet.

'Aren't you going to open it?' Chloe said.

When I'd come in that morning, she'd left a delicious pudding from Magnolia Bakery on my desk with a blue bow on top for my birthday. It was so sweet. She also insisted on organising my birthday drinks that evening, although I had no idea who'd come. After a few moments, I succumbed to the pressure from her and Brian and opened the box and pulled out each item, one by one. There was a red teapot, two red mugs, a packet of Yorkshire Tea, a bottle of Robinson's Orange Squash and an Aero Mint chocolate bar. At the bottom of the box was a card:

Tea is for the mornings, squash is for the morning after and
the chocolate is because I miss going out to buy you chocolate.
Francis xxx

Our break-up was both gradual and sudden. I'd already spent a couple of months flying back and forth between New York, and each time I'd spend longer there and leave more of my belongings behind. For Easter Weekend, I flew back to London so I could help Francis move out of our flat. I'd already taken most of my clothes and left him with the furniture and household items. Before that weekend, we'd loosely been keeping in touch over Skype, although Francis lamented on a call, 'Whenever I talk to you, you're hungover.' I found this irritating and avoided speaking to him too often.

He'd booked a trip to come and see me in the summer as part of the pretence that we were going to stay together once I'd moved to New York. One day, I said to him, 'I've got the type of visa where if we got married, you could come and live in New York, too.'

'I'd never want to live in New York,' he said.

'Okay, cool.' I walked back out of the room.

When I was at school, my friends would call my dad's car 'The Harry Potter Car' because he was always so quick to pick us up. My dad, true to form, came in his car to help Francis and me move flat. We drove Francis and all his things into his new flat, which he was moving into with a colleague from work. The table and benches went with him but they didn't fit in his new place so he had to cut them up, which was sad. The original plan was to leave my bike at his for when I flew back to London and stayed with him. Once everything was moved, my dad waited in the car outside and Francis and I sat on the sofa in his new place.

'I should probably take my bike.'

'Yeah.' He was looking down at the floor.

'Um, this is probably it, isn't it?' I said.

'Yeah.'

We sat there for a moment in silence. He was still looking down at the floor. Although he was avoiding my gaze, he didn't seem particularly upset. My pride wanted him to put up a bit more of a fight. He looked up at me, 'Can I still hang out with your friends?'

'Are you fucking kidding me?'

This was a sore spot for me. It was the paranoia I'd had with Richard that he liked my friends more than he liked me, the anxiety that meant I told him not to come with me to Durham and if I'd let him come on that trip then maybe he'd still be alive. Francis asking to hang out with my friends fuelled both my insecurity and my guilt about the consequences of me being so stupidly insecure. Rage, the only emotion I could stomach, washed over me and I got up. It was time to leave. Francis helped me take my bike out to my dad's car. We said goodbye with an awkward hug and my dad, without comment, drove me and my bike back to East Finchley. My flight to New York, where I now lived, was the next day.

My relationship with Francis had been over for a while, possibly since before it even began. It ended for me one evening, while Daneal and I were having a pint in The Pub On The Park in London Fields. He said, 'I'm sure you and Francis could have a happy enough life together.' I paused as I let the words 'happy enough' hang between us. Those words told me that this could be it. This could really be it. All I could hope for from my life was to be in this relationship. The thought that this could be my life, a 'happy enough' life, gave me the push that I needed. Francis himself gave me another clue: 'There was something that clicked for you when you got home that day and you moving to New York was suddenly on the cards. You came home the happiest I'd seen you in months.' When he said this to me, I thought how I didn't recall him ever questioning or asking me about this lack of happiness he'd clearly seen and chosen not to mention or talk to me about.

In the months leading up to my move to New York, things had only got worse for me at the startup. I couldn't take it anymore. I couldn't take life anymore. Job offers were always finding their way to me and it was easy for me to passively be courted by another early stage startup and for it to get to the point where they'd offer me a job. This early stage startup promised me the world, as startup founders always do. They were going to be the next unicorn, they said; I'd work closely with the founders building this unicorn from scratch. I was seduced by them. Now I know that unicorns don't exist.

My job offer came, I wrote a letter of resignation for the hospitality startup, printed it out in the office and asked Tony if I could have a meeting with him the next day. Tony said that I should have talked to him about leaving rather than jumping to resigning. I got a lecture about how it's important how you leave a place, life is long, reputation matters and so on. I just sat there as I got what felt like a telling off.

Our meeting finally came to an end and Tony concluded he was going to speak to the main founder. Tony and I walked back to the office and he was still mumbling: 'Oh dear, how could you, this really isn't good.' He then asked if I'd signed the contract with the startup. I hadn't. They'd offered me a low salary and I was negotiating that with them but I didn't want to tell Tony that. When I dropped out of the job offer, they magically found the ability to offer me a lot more money, which is always the way.

Almost as soon as I got back to my desk, my phone started to ring. I looked at my phone; it was the founder. I took a sharp intake of breath and answered the call: 'Hello.'

'Tiffany, I just caught up with Tony.' He always spoke so fast.

'Yes.' It was always best to let him lead on the talking. My hand was shaking slightly.

'I have a request to make of you…'

'Sure.'

Could you work longer than your notice, so agree to give us six weeks, considering you have a trip to New York coming up next week anyway. Could you spend those six weeks working on the US PR strategy, so we have that from you before you leave?'

'Yeh, of course.'

I don't know if it was by their design all along, but I went on my trip to New York and started working on my strategy project. It was glorious not to be involved in the day-to-day management of anything and just be focusing on the project. All the American leaders were accommodating when I met with them, but they always asked, 'This sounds great, but who's going to execute on this?' At some point along the way, probably while wandering the streets of sunny downtown, I decided that I wanted it to be me who'd bring the project to life. It would mean me moving to New York and I liked the thought of that very much. Coincidentally, the US founder was back in London the following week; we went for lunch and as our ramen arrived, I made my case as to why he should let me come and be on his team. He listened to my little speech and simply said, 'Sure, we'd love to have you.'

'Oh, it's just English stuff from my ex-boyfriend,' I said as I was sat in the New York office and putting Francis's gifts back in the box, one by one. Maybe I'd got the story wrong. Maybe he wasn't so bad after all; he did once read *Wuthering Heights* because I'd said it was my favourite book (although I'm not sure if it is).

'That's classy,' said Brian, and the sound of his voice brought me back into the room.

'Yeh, I guess.'

I kicked the box to a corner under my desk, where it stayed for months. I'd stopped drinking tea in the mornings a long time ago. Now I lived in New York I drank black coffee.

Every morning, as I walked the streets of downtown New York, wearing my sunglasses and clutching my coffee, I felt as if I was the star of my own film. I felt an inner power as I pounded the streets of Manhattan and for my first few weeks in the city, I listened to Jay Z and Alicia Keys' 'Empire State of Mind' on repeat. New York had given me a rebirth and I was sold on the expansiveness and opportunity of the American dream. Shortly before my twenty-sixth birthday, I dyed my hair red and uploaded a selfie to Instagram with the caption: *New city, new hair.* I spent my first few months moving about unsold inventory at the hospitality startup, so I stayed in different parts of the city for free in New Yorkers' fancy apartments, which was incredibly exciting for someone who'd grown up watching films and TV shows set in the city.

I was falling in love and New York loved me back. Even though New York is full of people from England, I often received a reaction when I spoke and American New Yorkers heard my English accent. On pretty much a daily basis, when I was ordering a Starbucks, or a drink at a bar, the response I'd get made me feel like a celebrity.

'I love your accent,' people would so often say. And others in the line would overhear our conversation and look over at me, too.

'Where are you from?'

'London.'

'Oh, London. I've always wanted to go to London.'

'It's great,' I'd say, disingenuously, as I was delighted I wasn't there.

Similarly, I noticed that people listened to me more intently during work meetings when I started to speak, and my colleagues, who noticed it too, said that it was because of my accent. To the American ear, an English voice has an intellectual authority and I was told I had a particularly nice one. I had felt so terrible at my job for so long when I was in London, but my New York colleagues seemed excited I was there and interested in what I had to say, which boosted my confidence and I felt good at work again. I was also better suited to the direct style of communication in

New York. In London, I'd been told I was 'too direct'; no one in New York called me direct. I relaxed and felt that I could be more myself without being fearful of offending anybody because being 'too direct' wasn't something I did on purpose and so I didn't know how to dial it down. I also knew where I stood with New Yorkers and so my paranoia that had spiralled out of control in London melted away. I found New Yorkers were both friendlier and more professional and I came across far more senior and successful women than I had done working in London.

As I spent more time in the city, I began to wonder if the key cultural difference between the English and Americans is that Americans are all extroverts. Moving through New York was like being in a constant conversation. People everywhere were friendlier, chattier and more socially at ease. It made me realise how horrifically awkward English people, including me, even though I wasn't technically English, could be. If you met someone in New York, they'd just reach their hand out, without hesitation, for you to shake it. I was enamoured by this, as it was a far cry from the usual English little uncomfortable greeting dance of 'are we going for one kiss, two kisses or a handshake, or just a wave?'

Oh, how I loved New York in all its intense glory. I loved how the sun shone so brightly every single day. Looking back now, the shining sun might be what I miss the most about the city. I loved the heat of the summer and the snow in the winter. I adored the glamour of wearing sunglasses with a winter coat. I loved it all, even the sound of the sirens or the garbage on the street and the grittiness of the subway. I loved its madness, I loved its toughness and I loved how everything was more extreme than in London, which seemed awfully polite and grey in comparison. New York City had a fucked-up energy to it and it was an energy that was the perfect place to hide from my past demons.

Although I'd spent a lot of time in the New York office already, by moving there and becoming officially one of them, I wiped the slate clean. It was a friendlier and more relaxing place to be and life working in the regional offices seemed a lot simpler than the torment of working in the London-based mothership of the business. I no longer had a team to manage and so I wasn't responsible for anyone apart from myself; it was freeing to be released of any responsibility although I did feel a twinge of guilt for abandoning my team when I got dispatches from London.

Somehow, there were always people to drink with, all week. It was normal, expected even, to go out drinking every night in New York. I was used to binge drinking, but this 'at least half a bottle of wine every night' drinking was something else.

'How do you do this?' I asked my colleagues Brian and Chloe on one of my earliest days in the office when I was recovering from yet another hangover.

'You'll get used to it,' Chloe said.

'Welcome to New York,' Brian said and chuckled.

'I can't imagine getting used to this,' I replied at the time, but it wasn't long until my body adapted and I'd start my weekday mornings with a headache and multiple cups of black coffee.

My weekends were emptier than the weekdays. On a Saturday morning in June, shortly after my twenty-sixth birthday, I woke up and stared at the ceiling. As with every Saturday morning, I had nothing to do. I knew my hangover needed a black iced coffee and a cream cheese bagel as big as my face. I got out of bed and put on my New York summer weekend uniform, which was a pair of blue denim cut-off shorts, a white t-shirt and white trainers, and I walked out of the door. I was subletting an apartment for a month right in the heart of Williamsburg, on North 7th and Bedford Avenue, so it took me minutes to get my bagel and coffee. I sat on the bench outside the café, sucking on the straw of my coffee as the ice melted, and I watched everyone go by. I wondered where they were going. I checked the time on my phone and it was 11 a.m. I had the rest of the day ahead of me. With nothing to do, I thought I'd play the same game I'd played the weekend before and the weekend before that. The game was I'd walk the streets and when I got to a crossing with the stop sign, then I'd take a turn rather than wait for the crossing to say I could pass. The idea of the game was that I'd never have to stop walking or wait to cross the road and I hoped it would pass the time and perhaps even allow me to get lost.

After a long time of walking straight for a while, then turning left, turning right and ending up back where I began, I decided to end the game and walk with more purpose. I got out my phone, opened Google Maps, changed direction and headed for the Brooklyn Bridge. On the bridge, halfway between Manhattan and Brooklyn, I heard his laugh. I stopped and looked out into the water as people passed me by. I heard it again. Richard's laugh. *He's come with me.* A chill ran down my spine and I shivered, even though it was 34 degrees and the sun was pounding down on me. I turned around and walked along the bridge, back towards Brooklyn. It started raining, hard, like it only rains in New York and not like the rain we get in London. I ran into a bar on the corner of a street – I can't remember where – and I sat on a stool at the bar and ordered a whiskey with ice. I could never say 'on the rocks' with a straight face.

In July, I found a more permanent home in the city. My friend from school, Jo, who I'd known since I was seven and soon became like a sister, had a spare room available in her place, which she shared with another girl, Olivia. It was an old, but beautiful and spacious, two-floor maisonette in Brooklyn's Bed-Stuy, which was about 40 minutes away from my office in downtown Manhattan. This was considered far away by New York standards and when I told New Yorkers that I lived in Bed-Stuy, they'd often say, 'That makes sense.' I was never quite sure what they meant by that, but, over time, I'd grow suspicious of the number of New Yorkers in their twenties who were earning low salaries and could afford to live in Manhattan apartments.

We had a garden and ours was often inhabited by all sorts of weird and wonderful people. Jo worked at a trendy literary magazine and Olivia in the art world. I didn't always have much to say to our almost constant stream of visitors, but I liked that they were there and I'd often sit out in the garden listening to their conversations. I became fond of how New Yorkers talked about star signs, and particularly how the fear of Mercury being in retrograde united people. I enjoyed it so much that I began to almost believe that astrology was as true as science. When Mercury is in retrograde, you supposedly start losing and breaking things, particularly technological things. One time when Mercury was in retrograde, I left my cell phone in the back of a cab. If I told someone what had happened they'd look at me with earnest eyes and say, 'Of course, we're in retrograde.' I was dazzled by how many people from these creative circles predicted that I was a Gemini. 'Ah, you work in communications,' they'd say. 'That makes sense.'

My housemate Olivia embodied New York with her combination of cool, earnestness, ambition and fun, and in many ways she was the perfect person to live with to feel in touch with the city. Jo, meanwhile, was someone from home who'd assimilated herself into New York and so was the ideal tour guide as I navigated this new world. Jo was brilliant at collecting people and bringing them together, so there were always people to be around or go out with. It was hard to feel lonely in those times as I was surrounded by people; and living with housemates I liked so much helped New York feel more like a home. Anna C. also moved to New York at the end of the summer and having her there made it even better. We went to the gym together as we had done in the summer Richard died, but this time we'd go to classes rather than wandering around playing on machines like we had when we were younger. Anna C.

would always get to the yoga class earlier than me and be waiting on a mat, with one for me by her side and a couple of blocks piled neatly waiting for me, too.

Unfortunately, at around a similar time that I was beginning to settle into my new home, and although the New York office was a far happier place than London's HQ, it soon became apparent that my time had come to leave the startup. So much was changing as the company had continued to grow; my paranoia, which I'd abated at first, with time, had crossed the shores and I'd run out of fight. I stopped turning up to the office and no one seemed to mind. We agreed I'd be officially gone by February and, as the year was ending, I was terrified I'd be sent back to the UK. I didn't have a plan and the reality of my rash decision was beginning to sink in and it unsettled me. I couldn't go back to London. I just couldn't.

I flew home to London for Christmas and Bristmas (coined by Bristol University students) with my old housemates. In our group, we take Bristmas as seriously as a family takes Christmas. Our first Bristmas was in our house in second year and we've done it every single year since. I hadn't kept in touch with the boys much since graduating, but I always showed up for Bristmas. For Bristmas 2014, I was back from New York and the clock was ticking on how much longer I could stay there. I had two months to find a job that would give me a US visa, which isn't an easy thing to get, otherwise I was out. I'd lie awake in my childhood bedroom – the room I was living in when Richard died that summer – and think about how I couldn't end up back there. That year, Bristmas was at The Drapers Arms in Islington. I'd last seen Zac at a leaving party I'd had shortly before moving to New York and our friendship, although we didn't talk often, was enjoying a peaceful phase. Zac and I always found ourselves sat next to each other at Bristol gatherings and after we'd eaten our roasts – I had the chicken, he always orders the beef – I turned to him and I leaned in with my Rioja-stained mouth and cracked lips.

'You don't understand. I *have* to stay there.'

'Or you could just move home.'

'Stop saying that. I can't. I can't come back home. I'm *finally* happy. I'm so happy. Really.'

'Okay. I might be able to help, actually. But I still think you should just move back.'

'Really, please? Is there anything you can do? I really have to stay, I'm begging you.'

'Yeh, I'll see if I can get you a job at my agency's office over there. I think they said they might be looking for someone.'

'That'd be amazing, thank you. Imagine if we became colleagues!'

'I'll see what I can do.'

Zac sent an email, I had a 20-minute job interview when I was back in New York, and by the end of February I was walking from a different downtown subway stop to a different office, with a coffee in my hand and a spring in my step. I'd worked at the hospitality startup for five years and I couldn't imagine what it would be like to be the new person at a company. My new office was small, maybe about 15 people. Overall, my new colleagues were very friendly and I was touched by the welcome sign they'd left on my desk on my first day. I was on the lifestyle team and now doing the PR for a trendy hotel brand. I thought that because the hotel was cool, it would mean my job would be exciting, which was a gloriously naive thought. Overnight, I'd been transported to a proper New York job with real New Yorkers, and the world of PR, fashion, hotels, beauty and celebrity parties seemed to me what the city was all about.

As much as I loved my cool new friends, I'd taken a pay-cut from my previous job and it was a shock to go from having a senior leadership position with a team who managed the agencies to someone who was asked to do press clippings and a lot of admin. I'd rejected another, much better paid job offer at a startup, which has gone on to be ludicrously successful. It's constantly in the news and described as a unicorn and I often wonder what my life would have been if I'd accepted the job offer. As I do when I get carried away with what my life with Richard might have been like if he'd stayed alive, I try to tell myself that it probably would have gone wrong anyway, even though I don't believe it. I was also offered a decent share package with the job offer and those headlines taunt me for the stupidity of my decision. I told people that I wanted to try something different but, in reality, I wanted to keep a connection to Zac and I was aware that was the case at the time although I wasn't able to articulate why I wanted that. Although I was so desperate to escape that period of my life that Zac represented, I also couldn't let it go. Working at the same company as him would be a thread that tied me to home, to him and to the person that I both wanted to connect to and escape. Somewhere, deep down, I knew that I could only heal what was broken by connecting to my past, but this knowledge manifested itself through this destructive and bizarre career decision. Taking that job at the PR agency was a mistake.

I tried to alleviate my boredom by picking up a daytime smoking habit again and I'd go out with my colleagues, who'd often use the time to bitch about the boss. I thought she was fine, but I didn't want to be left out so I'd try to join in. I was far more bothered by the nonsensical rules, which others didn't seem to mind as much but they drove me mad. You weren't allowed to have headphones on in the office and I struggled with my admin tasks without the rhythm of music to keep me going. You also weren't allowed to wear trainers, which was another shock after the casual dressing that was almost encouraged in startup land. It made no sense to me that I wasn't allowed to wear trainers if my feet were spending the whole day under the darkness of my desk. I'd often come into the office in my trainers and stay in them with my heels placed next to me under my desk, ready to put on if I was told off. I never was. There was no kettle in the office, so you'd have to buy drinks from outside, which was so expensive and a total nightmare whenever I had a cold. There also wasn't the freedom to come and go, like we had in the startup.

The other problem was that I was terribly naive about the reality of taking a pay cut to work at the PR agency. I was spending money like crazy from the moment I set foot in New York. I'd got accustomed to debt before then and I was always going in and out of my overdraft and using credit cards. Pay rises at the startup made no difference as I'd expand my lifestyle and spending to fit how much I earnt. However, it was when I took the pay cut and went to work at the PR agency that my attitude to money spiralled out of control. I was on the back foot before I even started working there because I had to find the money to buy my share options for the startup. I hadn't even thought that the day would come when I'd have to buy them and save the money to do so. As the deadline to buy them approached, I was desperate. I asked so many people if they could loan me the money. I needed £5,000. I also didn't know if it would even amount to anything and so it felt as if I was asking people to gamble with me. Eventually, I took out a loan and so on top of my pay cut I had to pay £300 a month to pay it back. I had also accrued a few more thousand pounds of debt, which meant I was in a cycle of debt and spending. I was using my UK credit cards, which had terrible exchange rates, to survive in New York, and I'd frequently have less than $5 in my US bank account and still have one week to go until pay day. Anyway, maths aside, I'd spend as though I had more money than I did. I was in a constant state of consumption, from my morning coffee to going to get $5 ginger shots in the middle of the day to ward off our hangovers, expensive $15 lunches, snacks in the afternoon and then going out for dinner and spending at least $60 eating in restaurants and drinking lots. If I did eat at home, I'd order from takeaway company Seamless. It was normal to order three times from Seamless on a Sunday. It's just how we ate. If I tried to go to a supermarket, I'd end up spending a fortune on groceries too because I decided I needed such things as $12 'dairy-free' ice-cream. I'd forgotten how to eat without spending lots of money. The problem was getting worse and worse as time went on. Everyone around me seemed to have so much more money than me. My appearance was much scruffier than my glamourous PR colleagues and I was rapidly gaining weight from eating Thai drunken noodles in bed a few times a week. The fashion team tried to help me by lending me clothes for events, and I don't think it'll ever leave me when one girl was going through the racks of clothing at the back of the office saying, 'This won't fit you, this won't fit you. Hmm, this won't fit you.'

By my second summer as a resident of New York, my body and my finances were spiralling out of control and I was becoming increasingly agitated. Everything I'd come to escape was starting to bubble to the surface and I could sense it was catching up with me. Just before I'd started working at the PR agency, I'd found solace in a relationship with an older man who lived in the West Village, but one day, overnight, he vanished from my life. It's about that time he disappeared that New York began to turn on me and I sobered up.

I had a terrible habit of being socially anxious in New York. In some ways, I wish I could go back in time and act like less of a weirdo in certain social situations (although, I'm not sure if anyone noticed). I was always enamoured by the social ease of New Yorkers; it seemed as if it was only me who was nervous and self-conscious. My social life had been much easier when I'd been surrounded by friends I'd grown up with, and without that context and familiarity I found I had little to say. I didn't like my job and I presumed other people wouldn't either, so I avoided talking about it as much as I could. I'd tag along to events with my housemates and, because of my nerves, I got bored and restless quickly. I'd often stand in a corner like a lemon, or I'd sit on the edge of the group, maybe on the floor, or in someone's room if it was a house party, and feel my tight clothes cut into my skin or worry about too much of my thigh being exposed from the different angles I sat in my skirt. I'd frequently get up as though I was going to the loo, and run away, out onto the empty streets of Brooklyn that I didn't know and walk the silent streets to find a cab because I'd rather do that than go back inside and wait for an Uber. But there was one party that I went to in January 2015, during the depths of the New York winter, when I didn't run away. I was hovering on the edge of the party, by a window and finishing a cigarette, when I was approached by a young-looking older man. Bill wore round glasses which sat on his button nose. He was tall and built with strong arms, and he was wearing an adult's clothes of chinos, leather boots and a checked shirt. He worked in the art world with Olivia. I didn't understand the art world of New York and knew even less about art than I did anything else, so I was terrified someone would try to talk to me about it that night. I remember overhearing at a party once someone saying their favourite artist was Jonas Wood and I memorised the name in case I was ever asked who my favourite artist was (no one ever did). Thankfully, Bill didn't talk to me about art. He seemed to be tickled by my Englishness. He loved my accent and I was intrigued by his Southern drawl, which rolled with a delectable softness that was a glorious antidote to the harshness of the noisy voices I so often heard on the East Coast. He talked a lot and I could have listened to him all night. On meeting him, I realised how few people I'd clicked with since moving to New York. I suppose they call that chemistry. Bill rescued me, from that party, from New York, and he whisked me off to a fantasy land in the heart of Manhattan.

Although he was 14 years older than me, we acted like children who'd just discovered their best friend in the playground and we'd want to see each other all the time. We spent most evenings together from the winter to the summer months. I'd sometimes spend a week in his apartment in the West Village without going back to my own. We drank and fought furiously. None of it felt real. He didn't feel real. We'd meet every night at a bar. He called me 'Poo' and he'd shout 'Poo' when I arrived and sat next to him, and people would turn their heads. He taught me how to order a martini. We'd go back to his apartment and sit side by side on his sofa, drinking Bordeaux and listening to Bob Dylan and talking about our lives. Sometimes we'd stop and listen to 'Blowin' in the Wind' or I'd hang out of his window, smoking and looking down at the frantic streets of New York beneath my haven.

One night, I was in a bar with him and I was so drunk that I was slipping off my bar stool, but the whiskeys kept landing in front of me. I don't know what was said before, but I heard myself saying, 'I had a boyfriend who killed himself when I was 20. I never talk about it.'

'Poo,' he said.

I looked back at him. We were huddled so closely together that our noses were touching the whiskey glasses.

'Poo, we're all carrying pain. We're all walking through life carrying pain.'

I said nothing.

'I'm an old man now and I can tell you – we're all carrying pain.'

I sat up on my stool. Until that moment, it hadn't occurred to me that it wasn't just me moving through life suffering with my pain. That was one of the most important lessons he taught me. I'd felt so isolated that I genuinely thought I was the exception, whereas of course, in reality, as he said, 'we're all carrying pain'. My own experience of grief had destroyed a part of my empathy: it had hurt so much that I couldn't imagine how anyone could have experienced anything like it. If I'd known the truth – that everyone has a story – then my young life as a grieving person would have been a lot easier. I could have held hands with others and shared in our suffering. But instead, I suppressed it all, feared any feelings at all and presumed no one had any problems apart from me. This belief I can only attribute to a form of madness – a madness born out of a pool of shame, brought on by Richard's death and fuelled by the societal stigma around suicide.

Bill never met any of the few friends I had. Perhaps it was the age difference or because I didn't want to break the spell. The only person who did meet him was Evi, the girl who'd been my only female friend at Bristol, and the one who'd introduced me to Richard on my first night at university. They got on well, as I thought they would. After we left him, she said, 'He's like a character from a book.'

We'd been in each other's lives for around six months and one day, in summer, shortly after my twenty-seventh birthday in June, he vanished. He'd slipped in the pool at his friend's place in the Hamptons and had flown back to the South for surgery and decided to never come back to New York. I still had his keys and so I helped sort out his things and showed his apartment to some people who wanted to move into it. I lived there for a week on my own as a long, slow farewell to the place. But he was gone, it was my second summer in New York, I was alone again, and that's when the heart palpitations began.

When you first feel your heart beating heavily in your chest, it feels as if you're going to die. I thought that perhaps I was ready to die. The heat of the summer often made the palpitations unbearable. I'd lie there, willing them, begging them to please stop and go away. It was such a heavy beating feeling and it felt as if I'd totally lost control over my body. I googled 'I can feel my heart beating' on my phone and learned that it was caused by anxiety. I didn't know much about anxiety then, not knowing it would become a familiar friend. To this day, those physical feelings of anxiety have stuck with me and I'll forever know that it was an illness that moved into my body in summer 2015 in New York.

Day after day, I lay in my bed, begging the palpitations to stop. I tried everything I could think of: drinking, smoking, a Soul Cycle class. They wouldn't give in. I had no air conditioning and no money to buy any and so I felt as if I was living in an oven. One Friday, I stepped outside my apartment and onto the sidewalk and the heat of the sun seared through me. Sweat trickled down me. The noise hurt my ears: cars were beeping, people were shouting. I walked past a rat lying dead on the street next to a pile of black bin bags bursting full of trash on the street. I retched at the smell. I walked down into the damp and dirty subway. Now I felt as if I was really in an oven. The board which had never worked still didn't tell you when the train would come. I was late. I got on the subway and two stops in, a disagreement broke out between two passengers. There was always a drama, or worse, a performance. I'd finally make it to Soho and stop to buy a $5 iced coffee I couldn't afford.

'I love your accent. Where are you from?'

'London.'

'Oh, I've always wanted to go to London. One day.'

We had this conversation yesterday. And the day before. I waited at the collection point and pulled out my phone and checked my emails. It was my boss:

Are you coming in today?

Sent five minutes after 9.30 a.m. I replied with a simple 'yes' and walked to the office as slowly as I possibly could.

During my West Village romance, I'd pushed away most of the people I'd met before and so I didn't have much to do in New

York anymore. My social anxiety got way worse and if I met with a friend and he had some other friends there, I'd make excuses and run away again. If a friend came to visit me, I'd be embarrassed that I didn't have many friends for them and me to hang out with. Thankfully, I still had Anna C. I spent my twenty-seventh birthday just with Anna and Jo, a far cry from when I had my party a year ago, flooded with everyone I'd ever met in New York and at least 30 people there. I'd managed to lose friends.

I consumed more and more junk food and piled on the weight. I found comfort in Thai drunken noodles, red curry and burritos. I also lived close to Dough Doughnuts and would buy them and eat them in my bed. I watched all 236 episodes of *Friends* from start to finish and got wound up in the narrative of Ross and Rachel, projecting my own life onto that. Were Richard and I meant to be that or was it me and Zac? I watched *Gossip Girl* from start to finish too and got overly invested in the story of Chuck and Blair, again finding a part of myself in the messiness of their love and sexual chemistry. I was consuming all this junk and meanwhile I kept feeling my heart beating.

We had 'summer Fridays' at my agency, which meant we didn't have to work on Friday afternoons in the summer, and I hated them because it meant I had a whole extra afternoon with no plans and no one to do anything with. While my colleagues skipped off to their weekend locations and friends with houses in the Hamptons or Catskills, I'd go home and lie in the heat on my bed.

Then a cat came to live with us. From what I could gather, it was common for people to have fires in their homes in New York and Jo's boyfriend's flat had burnt down that summer. They'd found his cat in the ashes, hiding under a bed. The cat came to live with us and at first I was relieved to have a friend. The cat and I got on so well at the beginning and then, after a few days, my throat began to scratch and my nose became blocked. I'd be up all night swallowing and I soon realised I was allergic to the damn thing. Then the cat began to torment me. On two occasions, when I forgot to close my bedroom door, it shat in my room. It was a particularly grim hangover when I woke up to the smell of it. If I closed my bedroom door, the cat would wait outside the door for me and be there when I opened it. The cat would be the first thing I'd see in the morning and the last thing at night.

One day, at my desk at the PR agency, I suddenly felt a wave come over me and I began to shake. I got up, grabbed my phone and left the building immediately. I stepped outside onto the streets of Soho and marched as fast as I could. I was shaking, my heart was pounding and sweat was dribbling from my forehead. I found a bench outside an empty shop or something – I can't remember exactly. But the streets were quiet and as I sat on bench, I thought that this was it – I was going to die. I texted Bill, the man who'd once rescued me from the city, because we were still in touch. I told him that something weird was happening to me. No reply came when I needed it and I felt so alone. I didn't know who else I could tell and I knew I had to get back to the office. I sat there, on a bench, breathing in and out. A man walked past me and I saw a flash of Richard's face pass me by. *I have to get out of here.* I was still a little shaky when I made it back to the office. I sat down at my desk.

'You okay?' the girl who sat next to me asked.

'Yeah, I just went out for a cigarette.'

'Okay, cool,' she said and I saw her eyes look at the cigarette packet which was resting on my desk because I hadn't taken it with me and she turned back to her screen.

I knew I'd do it. I knew I'd romanticise the city. I knew I'd choose to forget what really happened when there. Not long after what I'd later learn was a panic attack, and shortly after I decided I needed to leave, I left the office in the middle of the day to go and get a piercing on the cuff of my ear. I wanted it to capture the sorrow of that time because I knew I'd forget. The hole in my ear was there to tell me not to run again. It needed to stop. They say the East Coast makes you hard. I'd say it broke me. My love for New York took a similar trajectory as my love for Richard. After a period of bliss, it came to a violent and visceral ending.

As I write this, I begin to wonder if there was divine intervention because it was merely days after my panic attack when I got a call from my friend who was starting his own startup and wanted me to come back to London and work with him on it. Everything moved very quickly and I left New York with the same impulsive rapidity that I arrived with. I left all my furniture and most my of things behind, just as I'd done when I'd left the flat with Francis, which I hope wasn't too annoying for my housemates. I crammed what I could into three suitcases and boarded the plane in September. I landed in London, pulled my suitcases off the carousel and put them on a trolley. I pushed the trolley through arrivals and then it occurred to me that perhaps I hadn't thought this through.

Chapter 12

Spinning

My prediction came true. Almost as soon as I arrived in the UK, I wanted to leave again. An air of malaise and emptiness settled in and I spent those autumn and winter months of 2015 sitting on my parents' sofa, watching the *X Factor* Saturday night after Saturday night. As I saw the hopeful contestants perform week after week, I was riddled with regret and had pangs for New York. After the highs of New York, being back in East Finchley was one big, long, tedious comedown.

I wasn't entirely sure what the point of my life was now. The pointlessness of it all moved into my bones and being at my parents' house took me back to a time I didn't want to go back to. I started my new job as soon as I returned to London. Daneal, my East London housemate from the earlier days of my twenties and a friend from Bristol University, had started a company with another guy our age. While I enjoyed talking to the two of them during the day, I wasn't fully engaged with my work and a feeling of apathy towards it settled in.

Within the monotony of my life, I found meaning and purpose in the sermon of a spin instructor. I'd enjoyed the odd Soul Cycle class in New York, but at $34 a pop, it was a limited pleasure. I didn't believe that London's answer to Soul Cycle, Psycle, would be able to repeat the full American church-like experience. At Soul Cycle, they'd say things like 'Have gratitude that you have legs you can use as you push your feet against the pedals.' I went to my first Psycle class in London with a few of my girlfriends and I didn't love it. I found it hard to keep up with the instructor and found the strobe lighting reminded me of those crap nightclubs that I hadn't been to since I went on holidays to places like Newquay as a teenager. But then I went back, got accustomed to the instructions and the room and found an instructor who brought that same American spirit to the class. What had started as a social thing soon became an obsession.

In time, I became one of those horrible people in Lululemon clothing who sits up off the saddle and starts bouncing on the bike before the class begins. My heart would burst with pride when my name was called out by the instructor, usually because she knew who I was since I was always there, or Tiffany is a good name to shout out loud in a spin class because it's easy to remember and sounds American. In class, I'd pedal away to Major Lazer, pushing myself with the push of the pedals, finding a release that I hadn't felt before. Sometimes I'd cry. I'd think about how beneath the emptiness inside me there was a depth of sadness. I'd think about the regret I had about Zac, the resentment I felt because Richard was dead, and I wondered if I'd slept with men with girlfriends because I wanted to steal from women what had been stolen from me. If I couldn't have my boyfriend, why couldn't I have theirs?

I'd also spend a huge amount of my time on the bike thinking about when I was going to be at the next class and how many classes I could fit in that week. One day, at the beginning of the class, the studio of 47 people I didn't know clapped to congratulate me for reaching my hundredth ride. That meant I'd spent around £1,800 in the place, plus more for the shakes after class, so maybe £2,000. The spin studio would talk about how we were part of a community, but I never really wanted to high five with the person on the bike next to me. Sometimes I'd go to class before work, sometimes I'd go after work, and sometimes I'd go with friends. I took Daneal one day after work and he commented on our way there that he could feel how excited I was about going to the class. My weekday evenings became an exercise schedule, starting with my yoga class on Monday and ending with a Friday night spin class. The endorphins kept me from dying from boredom.

This period of my life chimed nicely with the clean eating movement which was taking off over Instagram around this time. I wanted to be thinner; I'd always wanted to be thinner since I was an early teenager, apart from when I was in New York and too addicted to takeaways to notice I was expanding. I learned the power being thin gave you as a teenager when I morphed from the fat kid in the class to a more socially acceptable weight in the eyes of teenagers, and my social status shifted up the hierarchy. But my gravitation towards clean eating was about something far more sinister than wanting to be thin – rather than wanting to control my body, clean eating was a way to control my mind. I'd struggled with irritable bowel syndrome since university and although it was apparently caused by stress, as that's when I'd get the worse flare-ups, the clean eating movement led me to decide that I must have certain food intolerances. I lapped up with relish the content of these bouncy, shiny people, many of whom have since been discredited and revealed to have eating disorders. There was one cookbook I cooked from that had a recipe that I'll never forget: it was leeks fried with eggs. That was it. That was the recipe: cut the leeks, put them in the pan, add the eggs. Clean eating became a new way to occupy my brain through the mental obstacle required when cutting out certain food groups and introducing fake food replacements. The thought of many of them now makes me feel sick. I can't look at another protein ball or coconut-flavoured treat or cacao dessert that has that musty, sweet smell of forgery. I ended up primarily eating chicken, broccoli and sweet potato mixed with a bunch of disgusting fake food snacks for a long time. The fact this was called 'clean eating', as though we can cure our dirty insides with blueberries and acai bowls, was the saddest thing of all.

There came a time when spin classes almost became too easy and I wasn't getting as high off the endorphins as I had previously, so I upped the ante by starting to go to Barry's Bootcamp. The classes were one hour long, where you'd switch between time on the treadmill and weights exercises on the floor. There was an air of competitiveness and intimidation to proceedings and, before class, people would unashamedly be looking at each other's bodies. I'd see eyes flick up and down my torso in a way that I hadn't seen since my school days. I was at the Shoreditch Barry's Bootcamp, which was the one closest to the city, so I guessed that this studio was populated by the sorts of people who had done graduate schemes after university. When it was time for class, I'd descend the stairs into the Hades-like red room for a punishing, brutal hour of work. This was hard-core and I was in too much pain or busy negotiating with the buttons on the treadmill to experience the revelations or spiritual awakenings I'd had at the spin studio.

The Barry's schedule was designed for you to be there every day and I'd be there as much as I could, even though I was still in debt, living with my parents and on a modest early-stage startup salary. I was spending around £18 a day on an exercise class and I'd always buy the shakes after class for another £6. The brands of these places and the full-package 'community' experience, including the shakes, were a comfort blanket during a cold and empty time.

This was a very socially acceptable way to lose weight in 2015. Alongside the clean eating movement was the fashion for the toned aesthetic. *The Sunday Times' Style* magazine ran a 'fit not thin' campaign. It was official: the pursuit of thinness was out and the aspiration to be fit and healthy was in. It just so happened that those things would make you thinner, so you could still be aesthetically pleasing by society's standards. People were constantly commenting on my weight loss and toned tum and I was clearly seeking that validation because I wore clothes that showed my tighter physique, such as crop tops. I didn't recognise the girl in New York who'd been popping out of her jeans. Once I overheard a group of girlfriends at a party talking with a tone of admiration about how I'd lost weight.

I thought I was fine but others didn't. After some time in London, my social life slowly began to rebuild, often led by Anna S., with whom it was a joy to be reunited. She invited me out a lot and, over time, my diary filled out a bit more at the weekends, with invites to birthday parties and nights out. This was when my phone became a place of torture as I'd wake up the next day to messages from friends saying things like: 'If you ever want to talk, let me know.' This would add a layer of anxiety on top of the anxiety that already existed from my hangover. I'd try to remember what I'd said to prompt messages like these. I recalled not wanting the night to end, being back at a friend's house and being terrified that it would soon be time to go. I recalled rambling about how Richard's friends had turned away from me at the funeral.

There were some moments I remembered more clearly, like when I'd gone to the bathroom during a party with my friend Carly and she'd offered to help pay for therapy. I didn't think I needed it, but I appreciated the kindness and generosity of her offer. Perhaps it was too much exercising, clean eating or just too much booze, but my ability for memory recall was decreasing and blackouts were more common. Our investors had thrown a big Christmas party for all their startups and I'd learn that at the party, during my blackout, I started shouting at Daneal, who was still my boss, in front of everyone that he'd be nothing without me. I never quite recovered from the shame when I found out about this incident and it made me on edge for the rest of the time I worked there.

I may be forgetting, but my phone was keeping tabs on my unravelling and it was clear that something was brimming on the surface, eager to jump out of me and was beginning to spill out. I'd wake up and cringe over drunken messages I'd sent to Zac overnight, which were often slightly cryptic declarations of love with statements like: 'There are things that need to be said.' I'd wake up, read my phone and send apologies the next day: 'Oops, clearly wasted. Ignore me!' And he'd say: 'No worries.'

I think I thought Zac and I would get back together when I moved back from New York. Actually, that's a lie. I know I thought that because I mentioned it to Anna C. when we had our last day together before I left New York. She replied with a simple 'veto' and so I didn't want to talk to her about it further.

Year after year, in September, Zac and I were brought together by our mutual friend's birthday party and this was the first time I'd seen him since I'd moved back to London in September 2015. When I was outside the pub, he came out, came up to me and said, 'Did you get my WhatsApp message?'

'No, what did it say?'

'Nothing.' He looked very uncomfortable.

'I didn't get anything, I changed from my US to my UK number.'

He looked sheepish and I was intrigued.

'Why, what did it say?'

'Nothing.'

'Oh, go on, tell me.'

'No, it was nothing.'

'Come on. Why won't you tell me? I'm dying to know.'

'It's nothing.' He walked back inside.

The moment I got home that night, I ran up to my bedroom and pulled out everything, looking for my US SIM card. I tore through the mess in my room, rifling through every item to try and find it. I eventually found the SIM card tucked into an old purse under the bed. I opened my iPhone SIM by using a paperclip, switched from my UK to my US SIM and opened WhatsApp. It didn't work. The SIM was out of service. I stared at it for a while. What had that message said? Why won't he tell me? Why had he wanted to take it back? I thought it could only be a message telling me he wanted to see me or that he wanted me to leave him alone. Depending on my mood, I'd think the message would have said one thing or the other.

I don't know where I'd got my hope, or even the idea that we'd get back together from. Up until this moment in my life, I'd floated, almost effortlessly, between love interests, even though most of them had been terrible choices. Perhaps it was being back in London and living in my childhood bedroom again that had sent me back in time. Whatever the reason, I became obsessed by him and for my first year back in London we were stuck in a toxic cycle and I was not the one with the upper hand.

There'd be times that we'd go home together and I could tell that these encounters were making neither of us feel good. There'd often be a performance beforehand that we weren't going to sleep together. There was the time at a friend's birthday when we'd gone on to The Lauriston in Kings Cross and Zac kept trying to set me up with this weird guy who was there. Zac would bring us together as a three and then immediately leave, as if he'd just taken the trash out. I ran away, found Zac outside having a cigarette, Zac would leave again and I'd turn and see the guy I didn't want to talk to standing there again. The guy eventually got the not very subtle message and, finally, I found Zac outside, he didn't run away and we got in an Uber together.

The pretence that we weren't going to sleep together continued into the early hours of the morning as we'd talk on his sofa. We'd frequently go out for cigarettes to break up the tension. On one of these breaks at four in the morning, Zac asked me an important question, 'Why are you always running away?'

'I don't do that. I just want to go back to America or something.'

'The thing is, you're always running. Ever since university. Except I don't get what it is you're running away from.'

'I don't do that.'

We were leaning side by side on a brick wall. He took a drag of his cigarette, turned towards me and said, 'You do.'

'Anyway, this is a stupid conversation. How about I don't run away tonight and stay here?'

'Sure. You can sleep in Dan's room.'

'Okay.'

The next mornings were always a horrible and awkward goodbye, and that morning was no different. The magic, along with my make-up from the night before had melted away. I could tell he wanted me out as soon as possible. In the cold light of day, I was very aware that I'd asked to stay. He was quiet and off with me and didn't offer me a coffee or tea. I've always noticed that when men want you to leave, they don't offer you a tea or coffee in the morning. Sometimes they offer you a hot drink in a half-hearted way though, which you have to watch out for too, so actually I prefer the honesty when they don't offer it at all. I got dressed, ordered an Uber and as we watched the driver inch closer to us on the app, Zac was itching for me to get out. I was relieved when it finally arrived and I ran down the stairs, shut the door and croaked another goodbye.

I put my sunglasses on and threw myself into the Uber. I wanted to put my headphones on and listen to music, but I worried the Uber driver would think I was rude. I stared out the window as the car whizzed up the North Circular from Willesden Green to East Finchley. I felt so dirty and so alone. While those gnarly feelings of shame disappeared when drunk, they came back in full force when hungover. I was self-conscious that the Uber driver knew how tragic I was. I also stank. It was 9 a.m. on a Sunday morning. When did I get so desperate? It was always me chasing after him, and the worst thing I always did – the thought of which cringed horribly with my hangover – is that I'd always ask him after sex if I was still the best he'd ever had. He always said, 'You know you are,' and for a moment, any power I might have had with the answer was lost by asking the question. That morning, I knew that his answer probably wasn't true and I was embarrassed by how pathetic I'd been for asking it.

When I got back from New York, the dating scene had changed. 'Dating' wasn't even a word we used in London when I'd lived here before, and in my absence online dating had become more mainstream. In New York, OkCupid and dating were more prevalent and normalised. 'It's like shopping for people,' Jo had said to me one day. While in New York, I created an OkCupid profile where I said one of my talents was 'answering my phone' and I went on one date at a bar in the East Village on my way to meet up with some colleagues on a Friday. My first ever online date was a bizarre experience. I found it curious how we never acknowledged that we met online or that it was a date. We sat at the bar, he paid for the beers and we had a conversation which felt as if it was going around in circles. He said I was cool and kept suggesting places that we could go together: 'Oh, I know this great Greek food place in Queens, I'll take you.' When we realised that we both smoked, there was a moment of relief that we could take a break from the awkwardness of being sat at the bar and having a surface-level conversation about our lives. I told him I had to go and meet up with other people, which was true. We parted ways with a hug and when I got to the bar with the others, people were excited to hear about my date, even though I didn't have much to say about it. But that one in New York was fine. It wasn't a big deal to hop into a bar for a couple of beers on your way to elsewhere. London, quite simply, doesn't have the geography for carefree online dating.

My first online date in London was a miserable experience. I was incredibly nervous as I took the tube from work to Holloway Road station. I was also already hungry. Travelling the distance just for the date lacked any spontaneity and I wished I was just going home. I'd gone on Bumble, which was the app du jour, in theory because you talked to the guys first; but in reality it was just the latest one people who I thought were most like me were on. It had been such a painfully long dry spell, aside from the times I'd pester Zac, and my life felt so empty that I thought I had to do it, so at least I was seen to be trying to do something about the lack of a love interest in my life. My work colleagues had been excited for me as if it were a big, life-changing moment that I'd taken this step. Daneal said, 'By the way, if this doesn't go well, that doesn't mean you should stop doing it.'

We met at The Lamb on the Holloway Road. I don't remember his name – it was probably something like Tom. He bought the first round, which meant I felt obliged to stay for a second. We talked about how I'd lived in America and he told me about some of his holidays in America. He told me he didn't like his job that much. We then talked about America again. I said it was a shame he didn't like his job that much. It surprised me as he was a journalist, but he said he wasn't the good kind. I then asked if he'd been to New Orleans and told him about when I went there. It was excruciating as I reached deep into my brain to find conversation starters; and yet, I wasn't sure how I could leave. I went to get our second round of drinks. I even stayed for the third round. I wondered if this was what dating was meant to be like – that you were supposed to break through this initial pain for some sort of reward at the end. I'd only been out with people who I'd known before and the idea of even being on 'a date' felt bizarre and unnatural. Dating felt like a job interview for a job I didn't want.

'Do you want another?'

'No, three is enough for me. I better get home. My parents will be wondering where I am.'

'Okay, cool, where are you headed?'

'I just take the 263 from across the road.'

He held the door of the pub open for me.

'Thanks.'

A second of silence, which felt like longer.

'Well that's my bus stop, just across from there.'

'I can wait with you.'

'Oh, no, please don't, honestly. The bus comes so often.'

There is a God, because next came the 263, zooming down the Holloway Road.

'There it is. I'd better run. Okay, bye.'

'Take care,' I sang back to him happily as I darted across the road and got on the bus.

I said hi to the bus driver, tapped my Oyster card and took a seat on the bottom deck. I got out my phone. I was amazed at how little time had passed. I breathed a sigh of relief and thought that there's no way I'm doing that again – online dating wasn't for me.

The most depressing experience of them all was the Shoreditch House incident, or maybe it would be more accurate to call it the incident at the Premier Inn in Aldgate. Although I used what I'm about to tell you as a funny story to entertain the crowd, the experience was horrifically depressing and made me feel like shit. Single people are so often treated as court jesters – it is our role, if we're incapable of finding someone, to, at the very least, have some horror stories to share about us trying to find someone. Anyway, here's what happened.

My friend Carly and I had gone to Shoreditch House on a Saturday night. I'd never really gone to a bar to meet men before and haven't since. We hung around the bar and smiled at passers-by while enjoying our drinks. We were joined by two guys. It turned out Carly had mutual friends with one of them because, you know, it's Shoreditch House. Carly and this guy, let's call him Joe, were locked in intense conversation and so I was left with his friend, who was a teacher called Charlie. In the haze of many vodkas with not too much soda and fresh lime, I thought he was pretty good-looking. Carly and the other guy told us they were going to dance. Charlie's bar chair and mine got closer and closer together and I was fascinated by all he had to say about education. I told him my opinions about what schools should be like and he listened to them as though I was very insightful. I felt we had a real connection when he told me that his school had started teaching the kids yoga: 'That's incredible, very inspiring.' Carly and his friend came by to say they were leaving together. Charlie asked if I wanted to explore. I had little desire to do so as I'd spent enough time there for work meetings, but I said yes. I followed him around from room to room and when we were outside, he pulled me in and we started kissing. When I stopped, and took a step back and looked at him, I saw that he had red wine spilt down one side of his white shirt.

'Should we go back to yours?'

'No, I live with my parents. Embarrassing, I know.'

'I live in Brixton, we can go back to mine.'

'Oh, I don't know. Brixton is kind of far.'

'Oh, come on. I'd like you to.'

'Ummm. Yeah, alright.'

'I'll go get us a cab while you get your coat.'

He found me in the downstairs lobby. He helped me put my coat on, we walked out and he opened the door to a cab and I got in. I was impressed by the smoothness of the operation, but that was soon to change.

'Oh shit. Oh shit.'

'What?'

'SHIT.'

'I don't have my keys.'

'Um, okay.'

'Shit, let me call Joe.'

'He's gone back to Carly's.'

'Gah, he's not answering.'

'Well, um, we can't go back to mine. Not sure you're ready to meet my parents quite yet. I'll text Carly to see if she can get Joe to read your messages.'

'Fuck, I really wanted you to come and see my place in Brixton. It's really nice. I was excited to show it to you.'

'Well, it wasn't meant to be.'

'We could go to a hotel?'

'Um.'

'I'll pay for it.'

'Okay, guess that could be fun. It's a real shame I live with my parents.'

'Let me look up one that's near here.'

By about the fourth hotel we'd stopped at and Charlie had got out of the cab, then come back to say no, either it was too expensive or full, it stopped being so fun.

'If you want, we can stop the cab and you can get out and order an Uber.'

I didn't want to wait on the side of the road in East London on my own at three in the morning. I was pretty sure we were in an illegal mini cab, too, so didn't want to stay alone in that one either, not that Charlie offered that as an option. The cab driver spoke up, 'There's a Premier Inn that I take people to.'

'Okay, let's try that. Thanks.'

We drove up to the Premier Inn in Aldgate. Charlie jumped out.

'I'll go check if they have availability. Do you want to sort the cab and I'll do the hotel?'

'Sure, how much?' I said to the driver as Charlie walked away.

'Um. Let's call it £80.' This was probably costing more than the hotel room.

'£80? Um, okay. I'll see if I have enough cash.'

I handed the cash to the cab driver and Charlie came out again with a thumbs-up and I got out of the car.

I sobered up in the harsh lighting of the Premier Inn lobby. I was wearing pleather leggings I'd bought from ASOS, a white shirt and these pointy-toed, pointy-heeled, high Zara velvet ankle boots which were unlike anything I'd normally wear. My black fake fur leather coat finished off my outfit. I didn't normally dress like this. I'd adopted a persona for the evening. I had hoped when getting dressed that this persona wasn't going to end up at the Premier Inn in Aldgate. I walked over to the vending machine and saw that there were condoms there, nestled between the Snickers and Walkers crisps. Charlie joined me at the vending machine.

'All checked in.'

'Okay, we should get condoms.'

'Let me get them.'

He theatrically stepped forward and put his money in the machine. A mini pack of red Durex Thin Feel condoms came out of the vending machine. He pulled them out of the flap and put them in his pocket. I avoided eye contact with the hotel receptionist as we got in the lift.

I was that horrible combination of tired and drunk and so I don't remember much of my first ever one-night stand. There was one point when we got into the shower briefly then got out of it again. At the end of the sex, in bed, my hair still wet and the sheets crumpled beneath me, I said, 'You have a big dick.'

He just turned away from me and said nothing.

I felt hot with shame. Why had I developed this habit of wanting to give a sort of post-match analysis after sex? I rolled away too and I was thankful the bed was big. I barely slept.

The next morning, I couldn't meet his eye because I didn't want him to look at me as I imagined I was an awful sight. No doubt my hair had frizzed from the failed shower escapade and I'd worn a lot of black eye make-up that night, which I suspected would be all over my face. I turned away from him and complained about my hangover.

'Uh, I feel so hungover.'

'Really? You didn't seem that drunk last night.'

This was a special skill of mine – to seem a lot more sober than I was. You'd think sitting in a cab for hours while we went from hotel to hotel with a total stranger would have been a clue to how drunk I was, but apparently not.

'Well, I was pretty drunk.'

'Sorry for that whole dragging you into the shower thing.'

'Guess you wanted to make full use of the hotel.'

I'm making this sound less awkward than it was. It was very awkward. We got out of bed shortly after we woke up and I walked around the room collecting items of my clothing. His phone kept ringing. We left the room and he left the remaining condoms in the box by the side of the bed. A single guy would take those with him, I thought. As we walked out onto Leman Street towards Aldgate station, one of the thin heels on my new, cheap shoes snapped. I stopped, he turned back and looked impatient and I continued walking, hobbling and mortified. He clearly couldn't take it anymore either and so even though the tube station was within our eye line he said, 'I have to make a phone call. I'm going to go to that Pret to make that call.'

'Okay, cool. Bye.'

'Bye,' he was already walking away from me. I realised he hadn't asked for my number.

Here's the most tragic part of this story. Despite this experience making me feel like such shit that I broke my shoe, I managed to find him on Facebook based on his first name and some other scant pieces of information he'd told me. I visited his Facebook page multiple times and I decided that because I could find him, he could find me and I spent weeks imagining that he would track me down and send me a message.

*

So, as I was sitting in the Uber from Zac's flat, I thought that perhaps this Zac situation was less depressing than that. Still, I felt awful, but I was in a love story in my head and so once the hangovers wore off and time passed and memories of the horror of the Sunday morning Uber journey had melted, I'd be back in the same situation again. Over and over again. For over a year, I was a moth to the flame and no amount of burning would keep me away. I tried to stay away but couldn't. I'd buy gig tickets for artists I'd never heard because he'd shared them on our Bristol WhatsApp thread and I knew he'd be there. My heart palpitations that had started in New York came home with me and their flare-ups were common. Now I was back in the land of free healthcare, I thought I'd get them checked out. I went to the GP and I was hooked up to a heart rate monitor for 48 hours. When I called the doctor for my results, he told me that nothing was wrong with me, so we left it at that.

April 2016

The email had CONFIDENTIAL in the subject line, so I got a shock while I was in the shower and my phone started to go off and I realised that other people would have got the same email. I'd read the email that changed my life in bed, gone down the stairs to the bathroom, leaving my phone on the side by the sink and that's when my WhatsApp started flashing up with messages. I came out of the shower and saw I'd got messages from my colleagues at the hospitality startup:

> *Your life changed today.*

> *What you going to do with it? Buy a helicopter?*

*

I opened the door to the kitchen; my parents were sat at the kitchen table, reading the paper and drinking tea. I'd been living with them at home for eight months and while it was a harmonious living situation, it was a far cry from the powerful independence I'd felt in my early days in New York. I was standing in the doorway in my towel.

'It's happened. It's sold. The startup sold.'

The email had the same flair for theatre the founder loved and it was at the end, after hundreds of words that there was the part that mattered. Please reply with your bank details and we'll transfer the six-figure sum to your account in the next few weeks.

'That's a lot of money for a young person,' my mum said.

'Now save it. Don't spend it. Be careful.' I closed the kitchen door on her.

I got to the office, sat at my desk and said nothing. Daneal was looking at me. 'Um, TP,' Daneal said. I looked over at him and on his screen was the news on *TechCrunch* that the startup had sold. We were in the same office as our investors and some other startups and this news was exciting. People came over and congratulated me. 'First employee, right? You must have made a tidy sum?' Daneal insisted we drop everything and the three of us went for a coffee at a café on Goswell Road, which funnily enough was the same café I'd cycled to that day I couldn't face going to the startup office in January 2014 and had uploaded the picture of my bike on Instagram. They made me pay for the coffees as a joke, now that I was rich.

'I'd be tempted to just not work for a while, but don't do that,' Daneal said.

'I know. I already did the maths and I could probably not work for ten years.'

I'd been in debt for almost a decade, which I blame more on the banks that lure students in with big overdrafts, than on my grief. All my friends in the first year of university had an account with the same bank, because it was the one which offered us the biggest overdraft. The news that the startup had sold meant that my expensive monthly debt fees and that consistent, anxious hum of being in debt had disappeared.

Other people were far more excited about my windfall of cash than I was. I didn't feel the rush of happiness you might expect. I didn't even feel relieved that I didn't have to worry about money anymore. I felt scared. I knew this meant that some sort of action was required of me and I didn't know what I wanted it to be. Countless people asked if I was going to buy property with the money. The amount I got wasn't enough to do that without getting a mortgage and that would be a struggle to afford on my early stage startup salary. In fact, if I had a pound for how many people asked if I was going to buy a house with it, I could probably have afforded the mortgage payments.

People wanted to know how much money I'd got and I didn't want to tell anyone. I felt shiny again, like I had in the Secret London days, and I didn't like it. At a work event, not long after the news of the startup had got out, a lot of people I knew came up to me:

'You look great. Is that all the spin classes you're doing?' I was wearing a cropped top with long sleeves and high-waisted loose trousers and heels.

'Sure.'

'Guess you can afford to do more of those now.'

The attention was on me and I felt shy. It was one of those nights where I kept drinking but kept feeling sober, the booze not filling me up.

I thought about when I felt happiest. I thought of when I was younger and sang in choirs and how when I opened my mouth to sing, my chest would fill with air and my body would feel whole and full. I'd always secretly wanted to be a singer. I found some singing lessons which were on Wednesday evenings at the Hackney

Empire. I thought I could do those before joining a choir. The lessons were with a small group of us and it was a bizarre collection of people who were all there for very different reasons. There was a Spanish student studying drama who wanted to move into musical theatre, a boy who sung in his church choir and a yoga teacher who was there because her boyfriend told her that he'd propose to her if she sang a specific song to him and she'd come to learn that song. I wondered if he knew that was why she was here. My reason, which I didn't share with the group, was to fill the emptiness inside of me with breath. We each had to choose a song to work on throughout the course. Without hesitation, nor a clear reason, I chose Etta James, 'At Last'. 'Excellent choice!' cried the teacher, bouncing with excitement at the piano. It really is one of the most beautiful songs in the world and I was too sad to sing it. When it was my turn to practise it in class, the teacher stopped playing on the piano. She stood up and said to me, 'You are terrified. You need to not be terrified, dear.'

'Okay.'

'This is a happy song. You've found true love. AT LAST. Sing as though you are happy.'

I wanted so desperately to embody the hope of that song and I listened to it on repeat. I tried and I tried. I listened to different versions of the song – Aretha Franklin, Beyoncé. I tried them all but I couldn't do it. Then I got bronchitis, I couldn't sing and I couldn't attend my remaining singing lessons. If there was ever a moment that I thought the world was against me, that was it. I'd tried.

I wanted to get rid of the startup money and I wanted to be somewhere, or someone, else, so I combined these two desires by deciding that I should go to business school in the US. The startup I'd been working at needed to pivot and there wasn't much of a role for me moving forward and so I found a job at a new startup where I could work for a year until I went to America to do my MBA. I had some time off before starting my next role, which timed perfectly with my sister's wedding in Cyprus. My dad, sister and her fiancé were flying out a couple of weeks early to have a pre-wedding holiday and make final arrangements. I changed my plans to fly out early with them and I was excited to be spending so long in the sun with my family. I found their company relaxing. My sister was very laid back about the wedding and there was a simplicity to enjoying myself while spending time with them in the sun. There wasn't any work in my life to occupy my thoughts or pull me away from the present.

When I moved back from New York, I had a lot of time and my sister was available to hang out with me and so she did, a lot. It was a joyous time of rediscovering each other and building a friendship. She'd played the big sister role of making my dinner and looking after me at school, but I always thought we were worlds apart. She was far more academic and studious and I saw myself as wilder and more rebellious. It was the first time in my life when I realised that despite a lifetime of denial and attempts to define myself against her, we were actually very similar. Every Monday, we'd go to a yoga class together and our bodies were restricted in the same ways and our measurements for the bike in spin class were the same as each other's, too. We'd go for dinner after our classes and when we swapped stories from our work, I realised that there were certain personality traits and views on the world that we shared. Elements of my personality, which had sometimes got me in trouble, became less alienating as I learned that they were family traits.

When I lived in New York, I felt a pang when I knew I was missing out on my sister's wedding preparations and so I was relieved that I moved back in time to take part. My sister asked me to be the chief bridesmaid and I was touched that I'd been given such an important role. She went out of her way to include me and make me feel part of the whole affair. We'd always been a little twosome; my mum complained that when we were young, we'd gang up against her and, as adults, not much had changed. The preparation for my sister's wedding gave us a focus to spend time together, too, and our weekends would fill with wedding dress shopping. There was a light-heartedness to it all, no one was taking the event too seriously and the bridezilla driven mad by stress that I was used to seeing on the reality TV shows I'd watch never came to be. The preparation for the wedding was fun, but I'd never quite got the point of weddings until the multi-day celebration for my sister's wedding begun.

The wedding was an international affair as my sister was marrying an American and she'd lived abroad a couple of times, so people flew in from all over the world. There was something about people from all over the world descending on this small island my father was from that gave the occasion a sense of connectedness and grandeur. My sister said she was surprised at how many people had said yes to coming all the way to Cyprus for the wedding and so it turned out that people loved the excuse for a party and a holiday. I felt part of a large, international family unit and my sense of belonging was far from the feelings of isolation and rejection I'd felt in my grief. My jobs as a bridesmaid also gave me a strong purpose and one which felt more meaningful than any of the startup work I'd done. The whole event was bursting with joy and fun. We spent time with our Irish cousins who we hadn't seen much since we were kids, and I made new friends, too. We all got to know each other over the days, and the constant sun, joy and celebration made these some of the happiest days of my life. I learned why weddings are so important to people. It isn't what they are but what they create: a large, familial, joyful gathering to celebrate love and family.

Some of the older people seemed worried about me and asked if I was okay during the wedding reception or went out of their way to tell me that I looked nice. I can only presume they thought as a single sister that I would be struggling watching my sister get married. Far from it, I approached all the festivities with full-hearted enthusiasm and on day three of the celebrations I was dancing on the rooftop of a boat with my new friends. I loved being around family and all the people and the celebration. I enjoyed myself, I got closer to my family and I had my plan for when I got back. Everything was going to be okay, I just needed to pass the business school exam.

The dreaded Graduate Management Admission Test (GMAT) is the first step in the application for business school and is famously hard. It requires high scores in English and maths, which my privileged education had not set me up for. It's also a test of stamina – the exam lasts four hours – and, just like business school, it's very expensive. The books cost hundreds of pounds and are updated every year, so you feel compelled to buy the latest versions to 'elevate yourself from the pack,' as the GMAT website puts it.

Over time, I worked to make my GMAT scores good enough. I quit drinking. I became a 'morning person' and squeezed in hours of study before work. The exam was all I thought about, day and night. I resented the 14-year-old me who had paid no attention in maths classes 13 years earlier. I told people how fun it was to be learning again.

Everyone takes the GMAT exam multiple times; you pay £200 each try, and you only need to submit your highest score, without revealing how many times you've already taken it. The first time I took the exam, I did badly, but that was to be expected – the first test is always a practice run, partly to test your ability to concentrate. The second time round, I thought I had it in the bag and was bursting with excitement as I rode the tube, ready for my second shot and dreaming of my new life. That year, the startup I was working for had been added as a case study for a course at Harvard Business School. I fantasised about the moment I'd raise my hand and announce to the class that I'd experienced this business problem first-hand. After four hours in a dingy exam centre in Holborn, business school would be mine.

I left my carefully planned energising snacks in a locker and went into the exam room. I sat down in front of a computer that looked like the ones that used to sit in the corner of school classrooms in the 1990s, and confidently started answering the multiple-choice questions. I was moving quickly through them and thought it was going well.

As soon as I'd completed the test, my final score flashed up on the screen. It was not good enough. It was really, really bad. I sat still in my seat and re-read the numbers, paralysed. If I just sit here and keep re-reading the numbers, I thought, maybe they'll change. Eventually, I slowly got up from my seat and walked past people who looked as if they were doing well. They were tidy-looking people, the sort of people who wore 'business casual' attire. The sort who left university with a place on a graduate scheme for a prestigious bank or consulting firm. Not people like me who wandered aimlessly through life without a plan.

To leave the test room, I had to hand my passport to the security guard, open at the page with my photograph. I started flicking through my passport but I couldn't find my face. Where had I gone? Where is my face? I kept flicking through the pages. My heart was racing and I started shaking. The guard calmly took the passport out of my hands. He said nothing, quickly flicked to the page with my photo and scanned it.

'Better luck next time, eh?'

I stared blankly back at him.

'You can always take it again you know, dear.' He handed me back my passport.

'No,' I said. 'No. I can't.'

I can't put myself through this again. I just know I can't. I go to my locker and I take out my bag. They all know. Each of these people.

They can see I've just messed this up. I can feel their eyes burning into me. They know I'm too stupid. I know I'm too stupid. Everyone knows I'm too stupid. I walk out of the building, embarrassed.

I step outside and the heat of the sun slaps me in the face. It's bright and harsh. Of course I'm not good enough – how could I be so foolish? Business school is for people with glossy hair, straight, white teeth and parents with second homes. It's for people who are actually clever – it's not for people like me.

I look up and I'm lost. I take out my phone and open Google Maps. *Where the fuck is the tube station?* I walk in a circle, trying to align myself with the blue dot on my screen. I start walking one way, but the blue dot goes the other, so I turn around. I'm walking in circles and don't have a clue where I'm going, even though I've walked this route thousands of times. It's a metaphor for how I'm lost in life, and it's really pissing me off. I need to find my way home. I just need to make it home.

I'm finally on the tube platform at Tottenham Court Road, and I'm standing a little too close to the edge. The image I had of my new life is crumbling. That girl who I thought I could be is on holiday somewhere warm and sunny. She has shiny hair and her laughter shows off her straight white teeth. She has a new boyfriend, who's sat beside her. I so want to be loved, but the image of the love I crave is melting. It's going and going. It's gone.

I'm left there on the platform, a worthless, stupid, nobody. I can't do anything right. I fuck everything up. Of course Richard wanted to leave me. No wonder Zac doesn't want me. I'm an embarrassment to my friends – I stay too late at their houses and ramble at them, because I'm too frightened to go home and be alone. Everyone apart from me could see that I was just running away and trying to escape. I couldn't see. Once again, I couldn't see.

I have nothing now. I don't like my life and I've lost my one-way ticket out of it. I don't like myself. People like me don't go to business school – what do we do? Maybe we step in front of a train.

My one flickering light has gone out. The train is coming. It's coming. I feel the motion of it passing me, and I take a step back. Richard is standing there. *Why have you come now? Why now?*

I know why. I can't even kill myself. I'm trapped in a fucking limbo where I don't want to live, but I can't die as I've seen what impact that has on the people you leave behind. I sit on the train as far away from people as I can. Why? Why has this happened to me? Have I not learned that life doesn't go to plan?

Images of the worst moments of my life come flashing back like a movie reel. The funeral. The black dress. I couldn't even give a proper speech that day. Pathetic. Why didn't I do anything more to help him? Where would I be now if he were alive? I'm so angry with the world. It's cruel and it's not fair. What I really want is for him to come back.

I give up. I've tried to keep living, but I can't do it anymore. I feel hollow, like an empty shell. I let him down by not even grieving for him properly.

I'm crying harder than I have in seven years. I'm crying harder than when I was on the train from Durham and had just heard Richard was in hospital. I'm crying harder than when Richard died.

I get off the tube at East Finchley and walk hurriedly home. Fuck, I have to face my family now. I'm not ready to face anyone. I've made such a fuss about this stupid exam and now I have to tell everybody I'm not good enough. It was a fool's errand and I am a fool: an unlovable fool. I want to go into my attic bedroom and curl up into a ball under the duvet until I disappear.

My mother is sat at the kitchen table. I don't say anything but fall to the floor, sobbing. 'IT'S NOT FAIR.' I'm screaming through my tears, but no words are coming out. It's not fair. It's not fair. It's not fair. It's not fair. It's not fair. *It's not fair.* Why me? The frustration is a ball in my chest and it's pulsating through me. It's so fucking mad. I want it to stop. I want to stop. My mother gets up from her chair and joins me on the floor.

'Bad things happen to my baby.'

She pulls me up and I sit on her lap on the chair. She gives me a hug.

'Your past is finally catching up with you.'

'I don't want it to. I really don't want it to.'

'I know. But it has. It just has.'

Part Three

Living

Chapter 13

Stirring the Pot

It had taken over a month for me to be sat in that chair. I cancelled once and then I cancelled again. I said that maybe it would be better to wait until after Christmas because I'd booked a trip to New York. I emailed to say that I was going to be travelling for work more than I thought. I said I might be moving to East London. She responded to say that it sounded as if now might not be the right time for me to do psychotherapy after all, but then added:

However, why don't you still come on Wednesday morning,
as planned, and we can discuss it then, with no obligation
to continue?

I didn't reply. The day before, she emailed to ask if I was coming. I replied and said no, because I was busy with work. I apologised and said I could come the following Wednesday. So there I was, sitting in an armchair and facing this petite woman called Jacqueline, who was sat in her own armchair a comfortable distance from me. She was younger than my parents, but older than any other adults I knew. Her hair was cut into a long bob with a fringe and was either grey or blonde, depending on how it caught the light. We were in a purpose-built room in her garden.

'I don't really need to be here,' I said.

She looked back at me as I readjusted my position in the chair. No position felt comfortable. Shouldn't a therapist's chair be softer? I looked around the room until my eyes finally landed on hers.

She looked back at me, right into my eyes. She tipped her head to one side, did a half-smile and raised her eyebrow.

I caved. 'There's this thing that happened to me at university that I've never really talked about and I think it's catching up with me.'

Jacqueline stayed silent. I squirmed.

I looked everywhere in the room, aside from at her, before surrendering again. 'I think it's making it difficult for me to, like, have a boyfriend.'

She stayed silent. She won again.

'But I'm fine generally. There's just this one thing I need to talk about and that's it. I don't need to be here after that, really.'

'Well,' she paused, 'my patients are usually in psychoanalysis for years.'

The word 'patient' hung above us in the air. I tried to do the maths of what that would cost: a huge expense for a service which, as far as I could tell, involved a lot of sitting in silence. I reasoned that the cost would still be cheaper than the amount I'd just spent on my eyes or my teeth. I'd recently had laser eye surgery and I'd just got braces, too.

'We can see how it goes. We can help you make sense of what happened at university, and we can explore how you got yourself into that situation in the first place.'

I flinched at the words 'got yourself into that situation'.

'First, tell me what happened.'

'My boyfriend…' My voice cracked as I tried to get my mouth around the next two words: 'committed suicide'. I didn't know then what I know now – to say 'commit' suicide is language from a time when suicide was a criminal act, like committing a crime. You're supposed to say 'died by suicide' or 'killed themselves'. But as the words 'committed suicide' came out, the tears came trickling down. I hadn't spoken his name out loud for so many years. I told her he was called Richard and he'd chosen to leave me in the most violent way when we were 20 years old. How did he even find something to tie that knot with? Semi-detached houses in Reading don't have long bits of rope lying around. And how could he have done all of that so quickly that it was done before his parents got back from Tesco?

I promised her that I was not remembering it wrong – we were really happy. He really didn't seem that bad. It's such an extreme thing to do. I don't understand it. Why would he want to leave me? It doesn't make sense. It just doesn't. And everyone at the funeral was looking at me as if to say, 'How could you not have known?' And they're right: how could I not have known? But I couldn't see it. I just couldn't.

'Well.' I noticed that she always tipped her head to one side before she talked. 'Why didn't they know?'

I stared back at her.

She continued, 'It's like… it only happened yesterday.'

I looked down at the floor.

'I haven't talked about it for so many years.'

I explained that my grief felt as if I had herpes. It felt as if I was carrying a shameful secret, an infectious disease that was bubbling close to the surface and could expose me at any moment. Something that if you got too close to me, you might catch. As I talked, she looked me in the eye and I couldn't quite believe the expression of sympathy on her face.

Then she tilted her head and said, 'We're at time.' It was as if she'd leaned in and clapped her hands in my face. I stood up with a jolt, gave her a broad smile and looked straight into her eyes.

'Thank you so much. Bye.' I grabbed my coat and bolted out the door, putting my arms through my coat as I hurried down the pavement. I pulled my phone and headphones out of my bag, plugged myself in and marched to the tube station.

My resistance to therapy continued. I told myself I would not become one of those people who starts sentences with 'My therapist says…' And once, I said to her, 'I'm not here to talk about my family.' If you know anything about psychotherapy, you'll know how ridiculous that is because talking about your family is basically the sole purpose of psychotherapy.

The truth of my resistance to therapy was simple: I was frightened that it would make me normal. Any success I'd had in my life had come from my hungry desire to fill the hole inside me with validation from others. My ambition came from my grief. I was scared that if that ambition was taken away from me, I'd no longer be special. But that same ambition meant that I now wanted to be fixed. The logic in my brain linked what happened with Richard to me not having a boyfriend now. Startups love to obsess over key performance indicators (KPIs), and getting a boyfriend was to be my therapy's KPI.

And so, week after week, I kept going back. I realised that I'd never be fixed – the best I could hope for was to learn how to let my body hold the scars. It wasn't long before I'd hear myself starting sentences with the words 'My therapist says...'

I spent hours and hours with Jacqueline going over what had happened, but I didn't find out why Richard killed himself. I made no more sense of what happened at all; we came to no conclusions, and there were no new insights or lightbulb moments. I learned nothing about why he did it. I came to accept that we can't always have certainty – not knowing is how it's always going to be.

I began to wonder if Jacqueline was a witch. She called it 'stirring the pot': the subconscious is awakened and matters from the past bubble to the surface. This leads us to confront our unfinished business. Her work breathed life back into Richard's ghost. I thought of him constantly. I saw him everywhere and I would hear his laugh as I walked down the street. It was a shock at first, but I grew used to having him around.

I sat on the bed I had slept in during the summer he died and welcomed the return of memories. Like that time when we were walking down Park Street in Freshers' Week and I was drunkenly and clumsily flirting, when I told him, 'I always get what I want.' Or when he said he was hot, I replied, 'Yeah, you are.' Or the first time he was in my room in Goldney Hall late one night and I was so nervous that I walked around pointing out pictures on my walls, and he followed me until I ran out of pictures to point at and we had our first kiss.

I recalled his first-year Halloween costume: 'Spatula Monster'. He went around collecting spatulas from the kitchens in our halls and stuck them all over his body before doing a dance, twisting from side to side, and we were all laughing, manically hard. I felt the rush of jealousy I'd once had when his ex-girlfriend kept calling him on Valentine's Day, late at night. He never answered. Fair play to the girl – I'd drunk call him on Valentine's Day if I could now.

I looked at his Facebook page, which I'd only done a handful of times after his death. I always found it so hard to see how frozen in time his page was and how his latest pictures were of us together, whereas my page had moved on. But in being able to go back and look at his page, I opened a treasure trove. Our relationship started in the days when one night out would warrant several Facebook photo albums. There's a whole album dedicated to a trip to the supermarket before a house party in our second year, with the trolley we stole to get all the booze home featuring heavily. I can't remember any nights that weren't preserved forever in a Facebook album.

Richard hated Facebook many years before it was cool to hate Facebook and he refused to get it at first. He was the only fresher I knew without it.

'But I can't tag you in photos, it's annoying. Stop being contrary – just get it.'

'I'm telling you, it's weird. I don't want it.'

'But it's, like, fun to add friends you've made the night before. Also, it's much easier to type messages on it than texting.'

He eventually got Facebook to make me happy, and now his page is a relic of our lives, including the last pictures of us together on a trip to Berlin with the rest of our house. Since I'd removed from my Facebook page that I was 'In a relationship with Richard', his page set him as just being 'In a relationship'. Time is frozen on that Facebook page, to a time when we were young and together and when my eyebrows were too thin from my over-plucking them.

When I began to thaw, I plunged to new depths of sadness and loneliness that I didn't know were possible to get to and still be breathing. It felt so unfair. I wanted him back. Couples made me feel a harsh, repetitive stab of loneliness. Twenty-eight is not a good age to have that problem. It seemed as if everyone else around me had easily found long-term, devoted partners. I found the weddings of people who had met at university very hard. I told myself that there is no alternate reality where he's still alive and we're still together, but that wouldn't stop me imagining it.

I'd fall asleep and feel him spooning me. I'd wake up in the middle of the night and cry because he'd gone. I'd call out to him and crave him desperately. I knew I'd be sad forever. I accepted that I'd never be totally fine and perhaps that was the most comforting thought of them all.

I imagined that we would be reunited when I die, and I still believe this. Me, the one who'd say that believing in God was like believing in Santa and roll my eyes and say, 'Trust me, if you'd been brought up Catholic, you'd get it.' Me, who never forgave that moment when I knelt down on the floor to pray and got no answer, or maybe I did get an answer, but it was just an answer I didn't want. I believed that Richard continued to exist, and his presence filled me with a warm rush. Sometimes, I'd speak to him, but sometimes I'd still be a bit pissed off with him, so didn't.

Going to therapy created conversations about Richard that I'd always been fearful of; but opening myself to the dead opened me up to the living. 'Just because so much time has passed, doesn't mean you don't still miss him,' Anna S. said. 'What you and Richard had was very special,' Anna C. said. These words meant everything to me; they told me that the magnitude of my grief was appropriate. Love stories so often end in marriage, but this is a love story where the person dies.

I put a picture of him up in my bedroom. This boy existed: please ask me who he is and I'll tell you. But the story doesn't end here, not everyone from the past was dead. I had yet to face some ghosts, and when you pick at old wounds, they bleed; and the healing process was far harsher than I could have imagined, as Jacqueline continued to stir the pot.

'I never knew you felt that way,' Zac said.

We were sat opposite each other in the garden of The Garden Gate pub in Hampstead. We always met here as it had a big garden and was halfway between his flat in Willesden Green and my parent's house in East Finchley. We were drunk.

'I'm looking at things differently now since going to therapy and my therapist said the funniest thing to me: she said that when I was talking about our break-up, the way I was talking about it, it was like it had happened yesterday.' I omitted that she'd said the same thing when I'd told her about Richard's death. When I told Jacqueline about what had happened with Zac all those years ago, when I'd ignored his warnings about the startup founders and I'd chosen them over him, I started crying and couldn't stop for a long time. I was shocked by my tears; the regret was so raw.

I lit another cigarette. I was leaning across the table and was very close to him as I continued, 'And now, it's all bubbling to the surface and I just feel so much regret for what's happened between us. I'm sorry about what happened with the founders of the startup and stuff and I guess I just always thought it was fine and we'd get back together one day.'

'I had no idea you felt that way.'

'Really? It seemed pretty obvious to me that it was obvious to you.'

'Well, you never said anything.'

'I'm saying it now.'

'I'm happy with how things are now.'

'Are you?'

'Yeah. You were so cold back then and now you're coming here and saying this.'

'I always had feelings for you, throughout it all. Can't we give it a go?'

'I don't know.'

'Surely, we may as well try. Like why not?'

I'd presumed we'd always get back together, so now I'd presumed he would just give me what I wanted in that moment, but instead he said, 'I loved you a lot.'

I ignored the use of the past tense and said, 'Okay, what happens now?'

'I don't know.'

'Should we go back to yours?'

Therapy is supposed to make you less crazy, yet on the way back to his I thought that this was it, that this was the turning point in the story of my life. I'd laid out those feeling things and now it was going to be this: Zac and me back together.

We went back to his and had the wildest, no holds barred sex we'd ever had. It was like my body knew it would be the last time and, like that, the past was put to bed. Sex was something that had always tied us so closely together and so it was only right that this was our farewell. Something magical happened that night, where, like an off-switch had been pressed, after that night, my desire for him stopped. I felt cleansed rather than grubby when I left his flat that night, and on some level I knew it was over.

We didn't speak to each other about what had happened that night and when we saw each other a couple of weeks later for Bristmas, we were normal and relaxed with each other. As with Richard, I accepted that he was going to continue to exist and I was able to make peace with his role and significance in my life. We'd gone to Oxford for Bristmas that year on one of the days between Christmas and New Year, and after we got back to London from Oxford, we went to the Edgware Road for drinks. Zac and I were outside, alone.

'What are you doing tomorrow?' I asked him. I have to admit, I only asked that because my pride got the better of me and I wanted him to ask me what I was doing tomorrow night. It took me a bit more time to abandon the 'disgruntled ex' routine and occasional naughty desire to rattle him. But after some time, I would talk to him about my love life, no matter how humiliating, because I valued his advice so highly, because he knew me so well, even though it was often delivered in a grating way: 'You think you're complicated, but you're not,' was the sort of thing he loved saying to me.

'Nothing. It's the boring bit of the year. Maybe see my brother,' he replied.

'Okay, nice.'

There was a silence as I waited for him to ask me what I was doing tomorrow. He probably saw straight through me and so he didn't ask, and I volunteered the information myself.

'I'm seeing Oliver tomorrow, actually.'

'What, *Epigram* Oliver?' Oliver hasn't been in this story since university days and so as a reminder, *Epigram* is the name of the Bristol University student newspaper and Oliver was the one who was the editor (when it should have been me). I'm over it now and yet I still can't resist describing him as such whenever I mention him.

'Yeh. We've become really good friends now. He's a nice guy.'

'Isn't he a bit boring?'

'You're just saying that because you're jealous.'

'Okay, cool. Hope you have a nice time.'

We went back inside.

*

'He's perfect.'

Jacqueline tilted her head and raised her eyebrow.

'Perfect?'

'Well, because he was there at that time and not like how Zac was there, but he knew me during that time after Richard had died and I was at Bristol.' I took a deep breath and began to explain to Jacqueline.

'So, Oliver is this guy who was at Bristol with me. He was the editor of the paper, when I was meant to be editor. Actually, I'm not sure why I brought that up or why that's relevant, but basically, we knew each other from the student paper. And when I got back to Bristol the first term of third year after Richard died, Oliver and I spent lots of time together working on the paper. Sometimes, or maybe it was just one time, we stayed up all night talking and we even talked about Richard once, which I hadn't really done with anyone before. I'd had a bit of a crush on Oliver, too, so that was confusing at the time. Anyway, so we were close and I had a bit of a crush, but then he started going out with this other girl on the paper and I started going out with Zac and before the end of the year, I dramatically quit the paper and Oliver and I fell out. Anyway, over the years we met up a couple of times and I bumped into him here and there. But around summer this year, we started hanging out and speaking all the time.'

I told the story the way you tell stories to therapists, always in a rush to get to the analysis part, while careful not to omit important details, but keen to omit some truths, too. The truth was, Oliver came back into my life through Instagram stories. As I explained to Jacqueline, how Instagram stories work is that you post disposable, carefree content from your daily life and then obsessively check who's watched it (unlike posts on the main Instagram feed, where you don't know who's seen them and who hasn't). I noticed Oliver kept looking at my Instagram stories and I seized the opportunity to contact him, so I messaged him in August and it didn't take long for me to suggest we meet up.

*

Oliver and I arranged to meet at The Flask in Highgate Village one Sunday afternoon. I arrived first and felt nervous as I waited for him to arrive. There was something in his face, too, when he arrived that made me think he seemed nervous as well. We kept getting drinks, each time one-ended, hesitating, not sure if the other person wanted to stay for another. We had those intense, electric conversations you can only have with someone who you have a shared history of sexual tension with.

We bonded over being in our late twenties and still living with our parents while everyone around us was settling down and buying furniture from Made.com. We talked about our eternal youth and how we were spiritually young. We got tipsier as the night progressed. The pub closed and we went home. We messaged each other the next day to say we were a bit hungover. Then we kept messaging. I was bored and lonely working at the new startup where the majority of the team were in Estonia, so I'd often be alone in a co-working space and feeling a thrill from messaging Oliver.

We met up a couple of times in sunny weather and drank beers and talked about how people were changing around us and we hadn't caught up yet. We were still muddling through while others were organising their weddings. He asked if I'd listened to the new Frank Ocean album yet and I immediately went to listen to it on repeat like a student studying for an exam on it. We talked about our love of Frank Ocean's previous album, where I exaggerated my own enthusiasm for it and he wrote out the lyrics to 'Thinking About You' in a message. He predicted Trump would win the election. I was sad when I saw he was right. In October, he wished me luck for my business school exam. I told him I'd failed. He was the only one who didn't say to me, 'Ah, I'm sure you can try again.' He said:

New life plan then?

Yes, maybe Berlin. Maybe anywhere. I downloaded the Duo Lingo app to refresh my German as a first step in my latest idea for escape.

Then, in December, I moved in with Anna S. into her flat in Tufnell Park. She and her boyfriend Bas were away in the bit between Christmas and New Year and so I invited Oliver round the day after our Bristmas trip to Oxford. While the relationship had become thrilling, I had also given up on expecting that anything would happen as surely it would have happened by now. We hadn't even come close on those nights in the pub where we'd sit a bit too close to each other. But just in case, I bought three bottles of red wine. We kept drinking and I was terrified the night would end, so I opened another bottle as soon as one finished. I'd just got braces and although they were Invisalign, so I could take them out, I still had ridges things on my teeth which were very visible and I was a bit self-conscious about them.

At one point in the evening, Oliver went upstairs to the loo and I waited for him in the living room. Then I heard a crash in the kitchen. I walked in and saw a pile of bowls, smashed on the floor, as if they'd just flown off the shelf. 'Is there a ghost here?' Oliver joked when he got back and I told him what had happened. 'I swear I was nowhere near those bowls.' Then I worried Anna S. would be angry with me for breaking so many of her bowls, especially how unbelievable it sounded that they just flew off the shelf. The only theory I could think of was that as Oliver ran up the stairs to the bathroom, he shook the house so they fell, but the breaking of the bowls still seemed supernatural and it freaked me out.

After the bowl drama, we were back on the sofa, then what felt like from nowhere and very suddenly, Oliver lunged towards me from his side of the sofa to kiss me. I put my glass of red wine down and kissed him back. I couldn't believe it after all this time and build up. I felt disassociated from the experience, as if I was watching it happening to me. I was terrified it wasn't real, so abruptly and prematurely, I suggested we go upstairs. I didn't want to discuss what was happening in case it made it stop. As we walked up the stairs, I tried as casually as I could to tell him I had my period and went via the bathroom to take my tampon out.

Then I don't remember the sex at all really, but everything moved quickly because it seemed as if it was going to end at any moment and I was wasted from too much red wine. But I remember him pulling out and there being blood all over the condom. I would later worry about that a lot as I recoiled in shame, but at the time, I thought it was fine because this was Oliver and he was perfect and he was cool about these things. It could have been the worst sex in the world and I'd have thought it was good because it was such an exciting thing to be happening to me.

I was then surprised again when he confidently settled himself in to stay over. 'Which side of the bed is yours?' Then he hugged me goodnight, rolled over. I put my braces back in my teeth and I lay there, wide awake, the adrenaline pumping through me all night.

The next morning, Oliver got up and left, saying he had to get back because he was going to his friend's house in the country for a few days for New Year's Eve. I was surprised by how he looked in my eyes and kissed me goodbye. After he left, I noticed he didn't take the book he was going to borrow with him. I went back to bed, took a sip of water and texted the Annas about what had happened. Anna C. said this made sense: nothing had happened before because we were both living with our parents. I had an obsessive level of excitement and on New Year's Eve, as I was getting ready to go out to a friend's 'Fuck 2016' themed party, he sent me a message on Instagram to wish me a happy New Year. I read the message and I ran down the stairs from my room to the living room to tell Anna and Bas about it. I was so worried I wouldn't hear from him and then I had. As when I saw him move across the sofa to kiss me, I couldn't believe it was happening. I ran back up the stairs and composed my reply. I didn't want to just reply with 'Happy New Year' – I thought that would be boring – so I gave it some thought, but wanted to reply quickly so it didn't look as if I was giving it too much thought, and I said:

Thank you! Happy new year to you too
See you in 2017.

I hoped the 'see you in 2017' evoked confidence rather than desperation. In the days that followed, I wasn't so sure. I went to the New Year's Eve party, which was naively themed around waving goodbye to a year of Brexit, Trump's election and the death of icons such as Prince and David Bowie. The hosts had created a big sign that said: 'Things Can Only Get Better'. We all thought this was a temporary blip of a year rather than what we see now – that 2016 was just the beginning of a seismic shift. Yet, judging by the number of 'fuck 2020' Instagram posts I saw on New Year's Eve 2020, I'm guessing we'll never learn. But anyway, although this was a politically themed party, I spent most of it talking about a boy.

I loved telling people the great romantic story of how we'd been friends for ten years (even though we technically hadn't spoken for most of that time) and how now it was happening: 'My time has come,' I said. Looking back, 'cringe' is not a strong enough word. People enjoyed the story for its romantic-comedy-style narrative and they were excited for me, and when we were ushered out of the party by the hosts in the early hours of New Year's Day morning, I was beaming the whole way home.

'So, he's perfect,' I told Jacqueline.

'Have you heard from him?'

Our friend Sam had come over to watch the Jonathan Creek Christmas special on New Year's Day and after I told him, bursting with excitement, about what had happened, he'd asked me if Oliver and I had been texting.

'Um, no,' I said, a bit embarrassed by my excitement to tell him about this guy who hadn't been speaking to me. By 5th January, it was becoming a problem and I didn't have the confidence to just say 'hi' like a normal person, so I did what we all do when we like someone and want to check if they like us, but don't have anything to say. I found a tangential thing to message him about. InDesign was the software we used to lay out the pages of the student newspaper, so I said:

> *Hello*
> *Just waiting for InDesign to download…*
> *Exciting times. Wonder if I remember how to use it*
> *How was the countryside?*

My memory is that it took him days to reply, but when I checked, he had replied the same day. Waiting for his reply must have felt like an eternity. I was miserable as I waited and Anna S. was in my room with me, lying on my bed next to me. I kept picking up my phone to check if he'd messaged and to re-read my message.

'Be careful!' She warned me. I didn't want to send a like to an old message or send something so he knew I was just staring at our conversation. While she was next to me, he replied. She told me to wait before opening it so he didn't see that I'd read it immediately. He asked why I was downloading InDesign, told me the countryside was fun and asked about my New Year's Eve.

> Tiff: *CV updating*
> *Obviously got it designed properly*
> *London was good thanks*

I think I sat on the floor chatting for most of it
This week has been a bit of a shock

And that was it. I never heard from him again. At first, nothing helped me feel better. I bored everyone senseless wondering why, even though I had the answer: he didn't like me in the way I liked him. A male friend of mine gave me the unhelpful perspective that sometimes, as a man with a female friend, you 'wonder what it might be like to sleep with them'. Anyone I told from Bristol said Oliver had a reputation for doing things like that, and the pedestal of perfection I put him on slowly melted away. I so desperately wanted him to be something he wasn't. I was also impatient for the work to be done. I'd checked into therapy, was that not the change I needed? But I know now that the work never ends and impatience only slows it down.

The rejection hurt so much and I understood in the weeks that followed why I'd shut myself off from feeling for so many years. To have the hope and the optimism crushed like that hurt like hell, but it only hurt so much because of the high I'd felt before. I'd experienced that life is more beautiful when you feel all of it. I'd also talked to so many people about my rejection that I learned that so many people had a story like this. To be burned by a crush is a universal experience of youth. By opening up to others, I learned that they opened back up to me and that did, eventually, help me to know. Rejection and heartbreak were part of life and it was an experience I needed to have. Oliver was one of my ghosts who belonged in the past, and my optimism came back with the hope of meeting someone new. I'd stopped escaping everything that had happened to me and I was connected to my past and to Richard and I didn't need to hold on to people from back then to stay connected to it. I can keep those memories of Richard alive while welcoming new people into my life. I looked in the mirror one day in January 2017 and I smiled. This is what it is to feel again and this is what it means to be alive.

Chapter 14

Celebrating Life

'I wouldn't want you walking away from this and blaming the company's culture. It's important that you hear that this is about you.'

I couldn't look my boss in the eye. I said nothing and stared down at the floor. Our co-working space had bright-orange carpets and all the rooms were walled with glass, so I knew people were walking past us and could see into the room we were sat in. It was June 2017, weeks after my twenty-ninth birthday, and six months since I'd checked myself into therapy, and six months since Oliver rejected me, and now another man was rejecting me.

He continued, 'And I want to emphasise that this isn't about performance, but it's about you.'

'Okay.'

The words he said when we sat down were swirling around in my head: 'We're not going to renew your contract.' He wasn't calling it what it was, but we both knew what was happening. My contract ended in a couple of months and I was working under the presumption I was staying beyond that time. I'd been excited for this meeting. The day before it, my colleague, who became the one who'd take over my work, told me he'd told my boss how hard I was finding working there, and when my boss came straight from that meeting to tell me he wanted to speak to me the next day, I thought I'd been vindicated.

'I can see it on you every day when you come in: you're miserable here.'

He was right, it was getting harder and harder to be there. Tensions between the team in London and the team in Estonia were growing; but still, quitting hadn't crossed my mind. We're taught not to quit. It made sense to me now why the team was so uncomfortably silent that morning as I presented the marketing plan for the next year – a plan I thought I'd be executing. They all already knew. That's why no one asked any questions. That's why my colleague, who was sat next to me for the whole presentation, stared at the floor throughout. The humiliation rippled through me as it all started making sense. I pulled on the resources I had had in me since I was 20, breathed deeply, kept my composure, looked up at him and said, 'It's a shame this has happened, but I understand. Thanks for everything you've done so far.'

'Okay. Now I really want to emphasise that this isn't about performance – we're happy with the work you've done, it's been great. It's about you.'

'I want you to hear this. It's about you.'

'Okay.'

'I want to make sure you learn from this. It's important that you learn from this for the next place you work. So you need to make sure you don't walk away from this blaming the culture.'

'Okay.'

'It's a trust thing between you and the team in Estonia. The CEO doesn't trust you.'

While I was being told not to blame the company's culture, I wasn't sure what else to blame. I liked the individuals involved at the company, far more so than many other people I'd come across in my working life; and straddling two teams across two locations would be a challenge for anyone. Blaming the culture is the kindest version of events I have; it doesn't place the blame on any individuals, and are individuals ever to blame for a company's issues? However, I was told not to blame the culture so I could make sure I learned from my firing, but I still wasn't fully sure why it had happened. Ultimately, the important lesson from that experience didn't come from considering where to place blame or from how I could have acted differently to keep my job.

Once the meeting came to a stilted, awkward close, I asked if I could go home. My boss said goodbye to me at the meeting room office door, so I walked back to our tiny office alone. As I was packing up my things, the CEO jumped up from his seat and came and stood next to me. I was terrified I was going to start crying, so before he had a chance to speak, I grabbed my things and ran out of the room. I took the stairs so I didn't have to stand there in full view waiting for the lift. As I walked through the corridors of the co-working space and past the glamorous women on reception, I felt like I had a 'just fired' neon sign flashing on my body. Once I stepped outside and walked a few steps down the street away from the office and on to Brick Lane, I burst into tears.

I kept walking to get as far away from there as possible and as I marched to the tube station, convinced everyone was looking at me, I called my sister. Calm and rational, like the lawyer that she is, she advised me to use this as an opportunity to leave well and on good terms. I was too in shock to process what she was saying. I couldn't imagine going back and doing more work for them. I got on the tube at Old Street and rode the empty carriage back to Tufnell Park. When I got back to my flat, it was 11 a.m. The world felt quiet. Anna S. and Bas were at work and I didn't know what to do with myself, so I sat on the living room floor. The room was bursting with books and items Anna S. had collected in the ten years she'd lived there. The room was full of a life well lived and I felt so terribly empty inside. At a click of a finger, my whole perception of my existence had gone. What was my life and who was I without work? The emptiness was shortly filled with the heat of humiliation. This wasn't a redundancy, this was getting fired, and as my boss had repeatedly said, I was to blame. I couldn't make sense of how it happened. I felt foolish for not seeing it coming. I'd done my work, they said this wasn't about performance and yes there were tensions between people, but I never thought they were that bad. Did I have a warped sense of reality? I couldn't see clearly what maybe everyone else could see. Did I just have a personality that pissed people off and I didn't realise that something was wrong with me? I hadn't seen this coming. Perhaps I was too opinionated, yet I'd always been praised at work for my good judgement. Perhaps it was because I didn't want the morning meeting to be until after my Barry's Bootcamp class because I'd said exercise was important to me. Maybe it was because I was a girl. I ran through it all in my head, oscillating between self-hate and victimhood, loathing them for doing this to me.

I'd probably only been sitting on the floor for a few minutes, but it felt like an eternity. I didn't want to tell anyone what had happened, but I didn't want to sit alone with my thoughts much longer. As the shame creeped up in me, reaching out to people saved me in that moment. I called Anna C. and we talked for a bit, but there wasn't much to say aside from the fact it felt confusing and horrible. Thankfully, I had my therapy session that evening, so I just had to make it through the day. Obviously, I had no food in the house for lunch, so I went across the road to Sainsbury's and bought a meal deal. The office worker lunch of a ham and cheese sandwich, salt and vinegar Walkers crisps and a Diet Coke brought me some comfort while I was in shock, grieving for a lost office life. After I ate my lunch, I moved to sit, propped up against my pillows, on my bed. I messaged my friend Claudia to tell her what had happened. She called me immediately and said with all the warmth in the world: 'No, don't be embarrassed. Don't be embarrassed. It's not about you.'

Since the business school plan had crashed and burned five months before, my approach to exploring other options had been half-arsed. It just seemed too difficult to get into the jobs that matched my interests. I had applied for a couple of political roles and didn't make it past the first round of applications. I had faced a challenge where I had a decent amount of valuable work experience, but to change careers and cross over to a different context would have involved starting from the ground up and I thought that perhaps I wasn't passionate enough to be prepared to do that. So, I had made the easy decision which was to stay at the startup. Maybe I wasn't supposed to make that decision; maybe they'd wanted me to leave and so I'd made things uncomfortable by asking to stay. But anyway, I thought I wanted to stay and yet, here I was, sat in my bedroom with nothing to do for the rest of the afternoon. I was too distracted to read or focus on anything, so I just sat there. Once I got to my therapy session, I sat down on the stiff armchair and burst into tears. I was surprised as Jacqueline appeared to be on my side because I'd spent the day convincing myself there must be something wrong with me.

Once the shock wore off, the anger came along and it was a rage so strong that I felt I was breathing out fire. The worst thing about getting fired is that it's not over immediately; like a break-up; there's a disentanglement process that's often wounding in its brutality. Again, as I find often happens in break-ups, there was a money dispute. It was quickly resolved, but it went on long enough for my rage to reach boiling point. I had to handover to the person taking over my work, while being suspicious that they played a role in my firing. I had to play nice so I'd not damage my reputation in the small startup world and get the money, so I felt at their mercy. Thankfully, they didn't make me come back in. In subsequent years, I worked with a startup that fired someone, then got the person to come back in for a couple of days for handover, which I thought was so cruel. I couldn't handle it. I knew how that person felt every moment they sat there.

On Friday night, we had people round for dinner and I ranted and I ranted. I downed the wine and I relished in the drama as I dominated the conversation by going round in circles. I enjoyed the shock of my audience when I told them that someone on the tech team had babe shots as his screensaver on his computer in the office. I felt validated as people shook their heads and said, 'I can't believe he said that to you.' My friends were good sports as I made empty threats and tore through my rage. Before the guests left, I went to my bedroom and passed out.

Once the anger had subsided, I felt empty and humiliated. Then it was Sunday night and I felt weird without the usual sense of dread I was used to feeling on a Sunday night. It was a funny thought that my Monday morning was going to be the same as it had been the last three days since I'd lost my job. As I went to sleep, I didn't set an alarm for the next morning, as there wasn't any point. On Monday, I woke up and began my new routine. I waited for Anna and Bas to leave the house before emerging from my room, because that seemed like the right thing to do, and then the empty house would be mine for the day. I'd start by making a pot of coffee and cooking scrambled eggs on a very low heat for 20 minutes. I was giving a speech at a friend's wedding that upcoming weekend, so I had that to focus on. The wedding would be the first time I'd be around people I didn't know since my firing.

I always find it terribly generous when the couple getting married sit me next to an eligible bachelor at a wedding. Many of my friends have gone out of their way to place me well at a wedding; and if there are no single men to sit me beside, I've had friends be kind enough to sit me with people who are fun and I share interests with. However, every time I have been sat next to a guy, who is often the only single guy, at the wedding, it has never led to anything. Nothing. Not even a sloppy kiss on the dancefloor at 1 a.m. or whatever you can hope to get as the only single girl at a wedding. And yet, every time I got to my table, knowing in advance that the man next to me was single and the couple thought I'd like him, I'd feel a ripple of optimism as I sat down and I'd turn towards them and say, 'Hi, I'm Tiffany.'

'Hi, I'm Adrian.'

'Nice to meet you, Adrian… Now, tell me, why do you think we've been sat together?'

No man has ever laughed at this joke.

'I don't know, Tiffany. What do you do?'

He, like the others, was attractive and charming. The single guy at the wedding is always attractive and charming and perhaps that's why they're single: dating is a playground for a single man in his thirties and it's only since I began to feel this unfair disparity that I felt truly slapped in the face by the patriarchy. The unfairness of the dating game as I aged bothered me far more than my colleagues with babe shots as their screensavers or when I was told that I should be cleaning the office kitchen. The questions at the wedding that are asked about the two single people are: 'Oooh, what's he like?' and… 'What's wrong with her?'

'Oh, I've just been fired, actually.'

An uncomfortable pause.

'I'm sorry to hear that. What happened…? Do you want to talk about it?'

'Yes, happy to talk about it.'

I tried to give him a light and breezy summary of the team's struggles, how it wasn't right anyway, how it's common in startups for people to get fired and how it was no big deal, all chill.

He said, 'You sound bitter.'

I looked away from him, reached my hand out and took a gulp of wine. I'd told myself I'd have a maximum of two drinks before my speech but I'd downed the last of my second glass and still had the rest of dinner to get through. By the time I'd put my glass back down, he had turned away from me to speak to the person on his other side. My kind friend opposite me spotted I was in limbo and turned to bring me into her conversation with the guy next to her and said to me, 'So, how are you feeling about your speech?'

When it was my turn to speak, I got up and walked across the room and past the long rows of people. All eyes were on me: the single girl, no boyfriend, no job, just got fired – I ticked society's checkbox for everything going wrong for me. The words 'You sound bitter' were ringing in my ears as I was passed the microphone and spoke into it: 'Testing.' This speech was for a high-achieving person; this friend ticked all of society's checkboxes: got a first from Oxford, a job at one of the top consulting firms and was getting married under the age of 30. I unfolded my paper, looked down at the words, looked up again, smiled and began. Performing to a crowd was my happy place. Jacqueline had told me that actors are shy, and during that speech I was talking about something and someone else that wasn't me, and the only feedback I got was laughter and applause. My walk back to my seat was bolder than my walk there. When I sat down, Adrian turned to me and said, 'Good job.'

'Thanks, I can drink now.'

And drink I did. It was a relief to break free from the seating plan and be reunited with my friends. I spent the rest of the night mostly with Anna C., who was my very fun watchful guardian for the night, as she had been so many times before over the years. At the end of the night, she batted away a creepy relative who'd tried to get in the cab with us, who I hadn't even noticed was after me.

'I see that ring on your finger,' she shouted at him.

'I'm not talking to you, I'm talking to your friend.'

'Get away from her.'

He backed off.

We got home, dissected the night's drama, slept in the same bed and got a Domino's the next day.

I didn't want anyone else to call me bitter, but I didn't want to lie either, so meeting people continued to be a chore. I wondered if reactions like these that I was experiencing since getting fired were what Richard had wanted to avoid when he'd read the letter from Bristol telling him he'd failed his year. I felt so wounded when people reacted badly. It was extremely uncomfortable in a social situation for someone to be deprived of the opportunity to get the measure of who you were if you didn't have an answer for what you did for work. I kept thinking that maybe Richard knew how judgemental people would be. Failing university, losing a job, any failure could happen to any of us, especially to those of us who try, yet it felt so catastrophic. Whereas I'd once felt successful and shiny, now it was like having a bad smell that I couldn't shake off.

I'll never forget how on one of these occasions a person I met said, 'What did you do?' when I told her I'd been fired. I admired her honesty by asking the question. It was far better than people acting awkwardly about it. Even more, I admired my friend who leapt to my defence by saying, 'Tiffany's too humble to say…' And he continued with a reel of all my successful achievements to date; he glowed as he spoke and I felt his warmth, and the girl then said, 'Wow, that's so cool.'

I couldn't bring my friends with me on dates to tell my story for me, and any conversations I had with men on dating apps took a rapid downhill turn if I didn't have a good answer for what I did for work. I decided to take a break from the apps as when I'd lost my work, I'd lost a sense of myself and I needed to find it again before I could speak to these people. My engagement on the apps had been patchy anyway after my crushing disappointment with Oliver at the start of the year. Since then, I'd had two brief flings with men I didn't even fancy, but they were fun to get drunk with. One I thought was a promising prospect because we'd got a late-night McDonald's on our first date; the other lived a five-minute walk away from me. Both men ended up rejecting me.

As time passed without a job, I stared deeper into emptiness. Who was I without a job? I had lost a future; even though a future at that startup hadn't been appealing, at least I knew what the future looked like. I didn't know what I was doing now and I had no structure to my days or life anymore. I'd always worked. Aside from the summer after university, I'd always had jobs since I was 14. Work was what I was good at. Even when they were firing me, they told me that I was good at my work. As with Richard's death, I never really made sense of what happened, which made it harder to move on. But unlike with Richard's death, no part of me wanted my job back or to change what happened next. I remember when Richard died, my mum saying to me that nothing would feel as hard after that, and she was right. While the feelings when I lost my job were like my experience of grief, it felt nowhere near as bad as when Richard died. Nothing ever did feel as bad as Richard's death, and whatever life threw at me, I was always armed with the knowledge that no matter how much I suffered, I'd come out the other side. If I could experience joy existing in a world without Richard, then I believed that I could bounce back from anything. When you lose your job, you lose part of your identity, and getting fired was humiliating, humbling, horrible and shrouded in shame, but it still wasn't the same: there are other jobs, but there aren't other Richards. I wondered if I'd found resilience in knowing that everything bad that happens isn't as bad as the worst thing that happened.

Having nothing to do: there's a terror in that. I'd never been the sort of person to have hobbies. I had friends, I went to exercise classes and I went to work. The emptiness shined a light on the fact that I didn't know who I was and hadn't connected with my interests. The routine of waking up to an alarm every weekday, deciding what to wear, commuting on a stuffed tube carriage and sitting at a desk all day meant that I hadn't stopped to consider anything really. By the time you feed yourself, travel around London and obey your manager's orders, there isn't much time in the day left. I didn't immediately have the answers to the questions, but now I had the time to ask them. One of the most helpful pieces of advice I got came from one of the Bristol boys, Jonny. He said that if it were him, he'd watch TV during the day and he thought I should do that. It felt wrong to do it, but I found a real thrill in the freedom of turning on the TV in the middle of the day. When the screen started blaring out of the black box, I realised I was now my own boss and I was in charge of my own destiny.

At first, I'd been going to Barry's Bootcamp in the middle of every day. I found that by the time I walked to the one in Euston, did the class and walked back again and showered, three hours of the day had passed by. After some time, I didn't want to give my whole day over to exercise and so I joined the gym across the road and started training with a personal trainer once a week and going by myself with a program the rest of the time. I still enjoyed exercise classes, but I wanted to learn how to exercise in a less punishing and time-guzzling way and it was nice to have someone to talk to in my personal training sessions.

In theory, I had job hunting to occupy me, but I'd more accurately describe my job search as playing on my computer. At school and at university I'd always preferred the extra-curricular activities above the main event of academic learning and I began going to events on topics I was interested in. I also started reading – not just reading the same book for months for only a few minutes before bed every night, but properly reading. I read one book called *Not Working* by Lisa Owens where the protagonist took a year off work and didn't achieve anything, and that made me feel a lot better.

I had the safety net of the money from when the startup sold and so I was fortunate in that I could take my time in deciding what I wanted to do next. I didn't know what I wanted to do, but I knew I didn't want to apply for random jobs and so I pursued creating a life beyond work with enthusiasm. The more I read and the more events I attended, I felt as if my brain was literally expanding. I was having deeper and more vulnerable conversations with people and I suspected that although perhaps without a job, I had less to say, I was becoming more interesting as I absorbed more of the world. I had time, energy and space to think, and perhaps it's not a surprise that as time went on it became less and less likely that I'd be going back to work in the traditional sense of what it means to go to work.

One of the surprising things about not working is how many people there are to hang out with during the working day. Between people with days off, people on maternity leave, people who were back in London for summer, I found myself well occupied socially. I was also fortunate in how many holidays I had in my diary. I had a trip to Romania with a girl crew and a trip to Slovenia I'd organised with the Bristol boys coming up. That year, I'd settled into London life and was more willing to commit to holidays with friends as I was no longer chasing a plan to escape to elsewhere.

Summer is a great time to get fired from your job, and a lot of the conversations that changed the course of my life happened in the warmth of the beating sun. One of these was I when was sitting outside the café in St James's Park with my friend Rosie, who's one of those friends it's easy to pass time with, and we were sat there for hours. Rosie was living in Jordan but was back in London for a couple of weeks, and the afternoon whittled away as we sat in the sun and I continued to think it really was a gift to be fired in summertime.

'Why don't you come visit me in Jordan?'

'Oh, that could be fun. If I come, can I ride a camel?'

'Yes, of course you can. We can go to Petra, the Dead Sea and the desert to ride a camel. It'll be fun.'

I became very fixated on the thought of riding a camel. The cynic might say because I knew it would make an excellent Instagram photo, but it became a symbol for me taking optimistic owner-ship over the course of my life. In less than a couple of weeks I was on a flight to Jordan. It was the perfect trip for that time. On holiday, you have time to have much deeper conversations with friends, and Rosie and I had plenty of them. We also had a lot of fun, driving around the desert, running around sand dunes and trekking around a near-empty Petra in the 40-degree heat. We slept at a campsite in the desert and we'd booked a camel ride for the next morning. As we got to our camels and I saw how huge they were, I was suddenly terrified. I'd never even ridden a horse. I got on my camel as it sat on the floor and then it jerked up; it had a false start and pelted me forward, but it tried again and up it got on its long, thin legs and off we went. I was so high up. Rosie had some baby camels attached to her camel, who came with us, and off we rode through the empty desert.

I didn't know what was coming next in life, but as I looked around me right then, I couldn't have been happier that I'd been fired. I thought of a former colleague I'd met with the week before my trip, who'd told me that he'd wanted to do what I'd been doing: 'Take time out to work out who I really am and what I want to do with my life.' Until then, I hadn't thought that perhaps my position was aspirational. This time off had been a gift. Losing my job wasn't a failure; the real failure is to stop being free. From that day, I chose living over existing.

I tried and failed exploring a few different career moves in the following months, but it turned out that the right thing for me to do next was the one that came the easiest. I was spending a Friday afternoon with my old Bristol friend and former colleague Daneal and I had a call with the founder of the hospitality startup scheduled. He'd emailed me because he knew a founder who needed some brand help and he wanted to introduce us. As we sat in the sun, Daneal told me how to turn this call into my first freelancing opportunity. The idea to freelance hadn't come to me before. My phone rang, Daneal smiled at me and I walked away to take the call. He said my old boss had told him what happened, and I told him that this opportunity was perfect because I freelanced now.

The founder kindly told me, 'I'll keep my antenna up for you.' He and Tony had taken it on themselves to sort me out and Tony soon found me my first branding workshop client. So days after Daneal had told me how I was now freelance, I had my first client and then the business just flowed.

Eight months later, it was a boiling hot day in June 2018 and the night before my thirtieth birthday. My birthday party was the following evening and I'd been planning it since I set up the Facebook event in April. I hadn't celebrated my birthdays until my twenty-ninth birthday the year before and I loved that party so much that I was excited to be hosting a proper party for my thirtieth. My hesitancy to celebrate my birthdays throughout my twenties had come from a mix of social anxiety and the memory that it was so soon after my birthday that Richard had died. I also found his birthday, every year, very difficult. I still do. February remains my least favourite month: Valentine's Day and the never-ending cold, dark nights don't help.

Before my twenty-ninth birthday, I told my friend Sophie that I wasn't going to do anything for it and she said, 'Nooo. You must. To celebrate birthdays is to celebrate life.'

'Wow, I never thought about it like that. That's cool. Into it.'

Our friend Jess chimed in, 'I hate the pressure of hosting, but I always think how much I enjoy going to other people's birthdays and so it's almost a duty to do something for your birthday for others to enjoy.'

'So true.'

I loved that. To celebrate birthdays is to celebrate life and it was my duty to use my birthday for that celebration. My friend Claudia had found the venue Pamela Bar in Dalston for my twenty-ninth and we'd had an after party at the Tufnell Park flat I shared with Anna and Bas. I enjoyed the night so much and I didn't even find

hosting particularly stressful. And for my thirtieth, there was a lot
to celebrate. In the past year I'd upended my life and I'd discovered
an inner calm. I'd stopped running, escaping and numbing. One
day, I realised I'd been living with Anna S. and Bas for over a year
and it was the longest amount of time I'd lived anywhere since I
was 18 and left home for the first time to live in Bristol.

Anna S. and I found a venue for my party in the downstairs of
a bar in Kentish Town and my parents gave me a contribution for
the bar. I was keen to bring people together as I'd started meeting
new people and making new friends in the past year and I was
excited at the opportunity for people to mingle.

The night before my birthday, I was standing at a grand house
in central London somewhere as it's where Anna S. had told me
to meet her because she'd got us tickets for a live recording of the
podcast The High Low for my birthday. I'd rushed there and I was
sweating. The woman on the door looked me up and down. I felt
the weight of my over-full black backpack on my back.

'Which list are you on?'

'I'm not sure. My friend got tickets, we're going to the recording
of The High Low.'

'Hmm.'

She flicked through her iPad. I recalled when I used to do that
job in New York.

'Nothing here.'

Another, colourfully dressed, high-heeled woman came over
and said, 'Can you step aside please?'

She checked in other, more glamorous and less sweaty people.

'Okay, I'll just ask my friend.'

I took a step to one side, messaged Anna S., who sent me
the confirmation, which I showed to the woman on my phone
and she let me in. It was early afternoon on a sunny Friday and
the place was packed with people standing around and drinking
champagne. I followed the signs to the cloakroom and spotted

signs to a smoking area. After I checked my bag, I went back up the stairs and hovered a bit until Anna arrived. We drank free champagne and sat in the front row of The High Low recording and took some pictures for Instagram.

'Can't wait for Zing tonight.'

'Same.'

'Should we hang here for a bit?'

'Yeh, Bas won't be back from work for a bit.'

'Yeh, it's such a nice day. Should we go outside?'

'Cool, let's go out the front.'

'I saw a sign when I went to the cloakroom for a garden. Should we go there?'

'No, I can't be bothered to go down and up the stairs. Let's just go out the front.'

A strong urge came over me and, in a move that was out of character, I insisted we find the garden. 'Come on, I want to find it. Could be fun.'

'Okay,' a hot Anna S. sighed.

On the way to the garden, we passed a huge champagne bottle decoration and I stopped to pose in front of it for a photo. We arrived and walked into a ball of smoke in the slightly overcrowded garden. We found the end of a table to perch on.

'I'm so excited for tomorrow.'

'I bet.'

'I'm just so excited to see who comes and if there's going to be any goss. I'm also excited for tonight. This is going to be such a good birthday.'

There was a natural lull in our conversation. Standing opposite me in my eye line, a guy was leaning against a wall, talking to a woman. I heard him say, 'I'm always the only single guy at weddings.'

I laughed and a little too loudly: half at Anna S., half at him. 'Me too, I'm always the only single girl at weddings.'

The woman he was talking to, heard me and turned towards us and said, 'Well, have you met Sean?'

Anna S. had her back to them, but she turned around towards them.

'Hi, Sean,' I said.

'Why don't you give this woman your number, Sean?' The woman he was with said.

He took a business card out of his wallet, a pen out of his bag on the floor, turned to lean the card on the wall, wrote something and handed me his card. I placed it in front of me on the table and said thanks as he and the woman went back inside. Shortly afterwards, he came back outside again.

'Can I join you both? That's my client, but she has some other people she needs to speak to.'

'Sure,' replied Anna S. and she scooted up to make space for him next to her. They were now both sat opposite me.

'So, Sean, you're always the single guy at the wedding?'

'Yep. That's me.'

'It's my thirtieth birthday party tomorrow.'

'Happy birthday.'

'Thanks. I've actually been looking for single people to invite to it because I've been thinking that it gets a bit tiresome being the only single person at parties and I want to bring people together so the singles can mingle. And meeting in real life is so much better that online dating, don't you think?'

It had been a few weeks since my latest online dating disappointment and I was still licking my wounds. The trouble I found with going on dates with people you actually found attractive was that they had more power to hurt you and I was still struggling with that fact. When I stepped through the doors of The Pineapple pub in Kentish Town and saw Joseph standing at the bar and he smiled as I walked towards him, I knew I was in serious trouble. I knew it so well that after our first two dates, I booked a trip to

New York with the Bristol boys that I'd been umming and ahhing about going on. My gut was right – by the time of the trip, things had gone wrong with Joseph and the trip to New York with the boys was the perfect ointment. But with each of these setbacks and mini heartbreaks, I became more emboldened because I preferred this choice to be living rather than existing. I began to feel sorry for people who weren't putting themselves regularly in the dating boxing ring; it's a wonderful place to practise the game of failure and resilience. I should have red-flagged Joseph when he said, 'It's pretty lame to be talking about your birthday party in June in April.'

But we brush over those shaming moments when they're so damn good-looking.

'Well, you have my number,' Sean said nodding his head to his card in front of me. 'Send me the details.'

'I will.'

Anna and I got up to go home. I could tell she was getting hungry. As we walked to the station, she said, 'I liked him.' Once we were home and full on our Zing takeaway, I texted Sean the details of the party.

The next day, I woke up and I was 30. I saw my family for brunch and then came home to prepare for the party. Anna C. had come round to get ready with me. I'd tried to find a new outfit to buy for the party but couldn't find one and realised it didn't matter. I wore a black jumpsuit I'd worn a few times previously, and before the party, Anna C. and I went to Franca Manca across the road for pizza with our friend Harry. I was buzzing with excitement and the three of us arrived at the venue and waited in the large, empty, dark room for people to arrive. We were sat there as a three for a long time. I'd started the playlist my friend Andrew had helped me make. I hoped I hadn't started playing it too early. Andrew and I had had a lot of back and forth about it, including when he said, 'Are we wedded to Meghan Trainor?'

I knew everyone was coming; they were just coming late because they were staying late. I've always believed that what makes a good party is the expectation that it'll be a good party. People show up with the attitude that they're going to play their role in making it a great night and so they do. Suddenly, it felt as if everyone arrived at once and the room was finally full by about 9.30 p.m. My family had come, including my two-month-old nephew: 'It's a good time to indoctrinate him into the Philippou party spirit,' my sister joked and I thought of how fun her wedding parties had been.

I floated about, welcoming people, making sure they had drinks and flitting between the groups. I gave the people who didn't know anyone the most focus and hardly spoke to my closest friends, who all knew each other. Sometimes, I'd stop and stand and watch over everyone interacting and talking.

I turned around and saw that Sean from the night before was standing there. I paused in shock.

'Oh, hello.'

'Hi.'

'You came.'

'I did. Happy Birthday.' We hugged.

'Thanks. Can I get you a drink? What would you like? We have beer, prosecco, red wine, white wine.'

'I'll take a beer, thanks.'

My sister came to ask if they should do the cake. She'd ordered me a ludicrously ginormous unicorn cake that sat on a table at the party. I looked around the room and it was weirdly empty.

'Where is everyone?'

'I think they're all in the smoking area.'

'Jack. Jack.' I called him over.

'Can you go and bring everyone inside.'

He nodded, 'Yes. Yes, I can do that.'

And I saw him march off on his mission. Within a few minutes, the room swelled with people again as everyone flooded back in. I stood by the cake and everyone started singing 'Happy Birthday'. I'm ending this story at a party because I will forever love a party. As everyone sang, I looked around the room: I saw the Annas; I saw Daneal, who I'd worked with at the startup; I saw my sister, dutifully filming it on her phone; I saw my parents smiling away; and I saw the new friends I'd made that year singing along, too; I saw Zac standing alongside the rest of the Bristols; and I saw the faces of so many who'd been there in the past ten years. Looking around this room I didn't know how I could have felt so alone for so long. These people had all been here, patiently waiting for my return to life. This is what it is to live. It's the people in your life that make life worth living.

Epilogue

The speech I wish I'd given at Richard's funeral

Dear Richard,

I wish we were back on Park Street in Bristol, browsing in the shops, stopping at our favourite café for carrot cake and sitting in the garden as the sun streams down on our faces and you let me eat all the icing. I wish that you knew how much pain I'd be in after you left me. I wish that you hadn't done it.

It will take me many years to understand why you did this, but one day I will. And when that day comes, I will understand that there was a monster in there that wouldn't leave you in peace. I'll understand your pain and the shame that was living inside you. I'll feel it myself. I'm so sorry you felt that way. I'm so sorry that our world allowed it. I'm so sorry that I allowed it.

I miss seeing you laugh. I'll hear your laugh often. I'll hear it on the Brooklyn Bridge. I'll hear it in the desert in Jordan. I'll hear it in a tiny bedroom in Whitechapel. I'll hear it all the time, and when I hear it, it will remind me of the joy that you brought into my life.

You once told me we were soulmates. It was the best thing I'd ever heard. I smiled and rolled over and I told you I agreed. I did not know that what you meant is one day you would leave this world to live in my soul forever.

If I had known that life was so fragile and that we were on some sort of time limit, I would have savoured every moment – nothing else would have mattered. It seems unfair that the love of my life would come to an end so soon. But I'm grateful that I had it at all. For you taught me what love is. You loved me for being me. Thank you for being so kind and loving.

You taught me something else: that this magnitude of grief is only here because of the magnitude of the love I have for you. I'll try to ignore it, I'll try to run and I'll try everything I can to escape. But you'll always be there – waiting patiently for me to come back to you and the person I was with you.

I don't believe in God. If there is a God, I don't like him much now anyway. But I do believe in you, and that you'll always be alive in my heart. When the day comes that I allow you to sit peacefully inside me, I'll see that what you have given me is a gift.

I'm going to make a promise to you now, because we can only change what comes next. I will not let you die in vain. I will not let others suffer in silence. I'll help others who are living with the burden of shame by telling my story. I will shout loudly about what makes life worth living. Together, we're going to tell the world that this must stop and it's time to focus on what really matters. As long as there is love in our lives, none of us walks alone.

A Letter from Tiffany

Thank you for reading the story I was scared to tell. I hope it stirred something in you. If you'd like to keep up to date with the latest news from Thread, you can sign up here.

www.thread-books.com/sign-up

Your email won't be shared and you can unsubscribe anytime.

I care about people living more joyful and purposeful lives and I hope this book has nudged you to think a little differently about your own life. I wrote this book because I wanted to use my story to tackle the shame and stigma that exists around suicide. I also wanted it to be a rallying cry for us to focus on what matters in life and I wanted to create something that would bring you both solace and enjoyment.

The reaction I've had from this book and saying my shame out loud has made me feel less alone and more connected to people in my life. I hope that reading this has made you feel less alone, too. I'd love it if you could help me share my story and I'd be very grateful if you could write a review on the site where you purchased the book.

Please stay in touch with me. I write regularly in my newsletter, The Tiff Weekly, and I'm on social media and would love to see you there. I also co-host a podcast with my best pal, Anna

Codrea-Rado; you can find it where you get your podcasts and it's called *Is This Working?*

More stories from me soon.

With love,
Tiffany

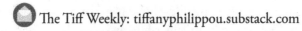 The Tiff Weekly: tiffanyphilippou.substack.com

@tiffphilippou

@tiffphilippou

Acknowledgements

It's the people in our lives who make life worth living and I want to thank all the people in my life who've played a part in this book's creation. To Anna Codrea-Rado, who's always had higher ambitions for me than I've had for myself. Thank you for always being on the other end of a voice note as I share every detail of my life with you. You're so wise and generous and I couldn't be happier that our work, our lives and our brains are so beautifully intertwined.

To Anna Steadman, for being such a balanced and consistent presence in my life since we were teens. I am blown away by the patience and love you've given me as a friend. Even though we no longer live together, I always feel at home when I'm with you. Thank you for being my trusted advisor as I've navigated the writing and publishing process – it means everything to me.

Thank you to my parents, Isabella and Glafkos, and my sister, Laura, for letting me write about you and maintaining good humour while I do so. Thank you for always feeding me and providing me with the solid foundation that allows me to boldly go out into the world and create.

Thank you to all the people who saw my potential as a writer; without you, this book wouldn't exist. Thank you to the wonderfully generous Rishi Dastidar, for having a vision for my writing career before I even considered it and for editing my early work and encouraging me to go to the memoir course at Goldsmiths. Thank you to my teacher, Anna Derrig, for coming up to me at the end of class and telling me to 'keep going'. It was the gentle, but powerful encouragement that I needed. To my memoir class buddy, Ally Kingston, and to the rest of the group, too. To Cheryl

Markosky for introducing me to my agent, Jonathan Conway. Thank you, Jonathan, for the unbelievably huge amount of time and dedication you have given to this book. Thank you to my editor, Claire Bord, for getting what I was trying to do with this book and for pushing me to keep delving to make it better. Thank you to the team at Thread for all your work on this book, too. Thank you for endorsing and commissioning me: Jo Livingstone, Vicky Spratt, Sarah Biddlecombe, Laura Jane Williams and Jillian Anthony. Thank you to my early readers and informal editors who championed me to keep going: Mairead Shenton and Andrew Naughtie.

Thank you to those who were with me while I was writing the book. To my housemate, Lara Enoch – thank you for being my constant cheerleader and all you did to make my life easier as I was writing the book. You're a true star. To Alessandro Lombardi, for being my 'head of recreation' and always bringing me chocolate. To all my friends who've read my writing and supported me. I see and appreciate all of you.

To the Bristol boys, because a lot of this was our story and I thank you for letting me tell it.

Thank you to Richard's parents for having the generosity to let me tell this story. Thank you also to Fin's mother. Thank you to Richard and Fin for the short but wonderful time we spent together; may you live on forever in these pages.

Finally, thank you to the children in my life: my nephew, Theo, and my godson, Kit. You fill my heart with so much joy and I hope this book plays a small part in helping young people, like you, not to feel the weight and pressure of societal expectations.

All my love, Tiffany xx

About the Author

Tiffany Philippou is a writer and podcaster and her writing has been published in *Stylist*, *Refinery29*, *Sifted*, *The i Paper* and *The Startup*.

She co-hosts the work, life and happiness podcast *Is This Working?* and the *Guardian* has said 'its look at mental health, productivity and even loneliness feels increasingly vital.' The podcast is a number one show in the UK Apple careers charts and is frequently in the top three in the business charts.

Tiffany also writes a weekly newsletter, about love, loss, finding meaning and some of the messier sides of life, called *The Tiff Weekly*.

She previously spent over ten years working in leadership roles in startups, and in addition to her work as a writer and podcaster, Tiffany works as a consultant and recruiter for startups.

Tiffany lives in London and her website has further information about her writing, podcast, newsletter and social media.

Resources

If you or anyone you know needs to speak to someone, you can phone the Samaritans in the UK at 116 123. For more information, visit the Samaritans website at www.samaritans.org

If you're in the US, The National Suicide Prevention Hotline is 1-800-273-8255

For information on suicide prevention visit the World Health Organization's website at www.who.int/mental_health/prevention/suicide/suicideprevent/e

CALM (Campaign Against Living Miserably) is leading a movement against suicide. See 'Get help on: suicidal thoughts', available at www.thecalmzone.net/help/get-help/suicide, and 'Worried about someone?', available at www.thecalmzone.net/help/worried-about-someone

GET CURIOUS.

Join our community

www.thread-books.com/sign-up

for special offers, exclusive content,
competitions and much more!

Follow us for the latest news

@Threadbooks
/Threadbooks
@Threadbooks_
/Threadbooks